# SHEDDING
# LIGHT
### ～ ON THE ～
# DARK SIDE

A GUIDE FOR YOUTH AND YOUNG ADULTS

# SHEDDING LIGHT

## ~ ON THE ~
## DARK SIDE

### DEFEATING
### THE FORCES
### OF EVIL

By

Stephen J. Stirling

CFI
An Imprint of Cedar Fort, Inc.
Springville, Utah

ISBN 13: 978-1-4621-1203-6

Published by CFI, an imprint of Cedar Fort, Inc.,
2373 W. 700 S., Springville, UT 84663
Distributed by Cedar Fort, Inc., www.cedarfort.com

LIBRARY OF CONGRESS CATALOGING-IN-PUBLICATION DATA

Stirling, Stephen J., 1953- author.
Shedding light on the dark side : defeating the forces of evil / Stephen J. Stirling.
    pages cm
Includes bibliographical references and index.
Summary: Discusses the nature and reality of Satan and how we can withstand him with the help of Christ.
ISBN 978-1-4621-1203-6
1.  Spiritual life--Church of Jesus Christ of Latter-day Saints. 2.  Spiritual warfare. 3.  Church of Jesus Christ of Latter-day Saints--Doctrines.  I. Title.

BX8656.S75 2013
235'.4--dc23

                           2013021997

Cover design by Shawnda Craig
Cover design © 2013 by Lyle Mortimer
Edited and typeset by Deborah Spencer

Printed in the United States of America

10  9  8  7  6  5  4  3  2  1

Printed on acid-free paper

*To Diane*
*the choice of my heart,*
*the love of my life,*
*the light of my world.*

# CONTENTS

*"And now, my sons, remember, remember that it is upon the rock of our Redeemer, who is Christ, the Son of God, that ye must build your foundation; that when the devil shall send forth his mighty winds, yea, his shafts in the whirlwind, yea, when all his hail and his mighty storm shall beat upon you, it shall have no power over you to drag you down to the gulf of misery and endless wo, because of the rock upon which ye are built, which is a sure foundation, a foundation whereon if men build they cannot fall."*

—Helaman 5:12

# Introduction
# THE LIGHT AND THE SHADOW

Throughout history Satan has been the source and mainspring of all evil. Across cultures, the world has found him both frightening and fascinating. This has not changed with the technological age. We live in an era of Facebook, Xbox, smartphones, and iPads. Yet, in spite of our sophistication, we should not be surprised that Satan is still the staple of campfire ghost stories, tales of witches and Ouija boards, and apocryphal yarns about body-snatching evil spirits or disobedient missionaries out for a swim.

Now, most of us have been there. We've told an eerie satanic story or two. And we've sat in huddled circles or lain in bed afterwards, trying to sleep with the light on, regretting the fear and the suffocating spiritual darkness created by these experiences. It's always pretty creepy.

The reason for these consistencies is simple: Satan likes the attention. He is, first and foremost, a disturbed exhibitionist. From the beginning he has thirsted for the hollow glory of the adoring masses. But, ultimately, he never lives up to the hype.

Jared was an intelligent, clearly uninterested student at the seminary where I was principal several years ago. He was a pain in the neck to his teacher and a distraction to other students. So, as principal, I pulled him out one day and we enjoyed a "father/son" chat.

"What's wrong with you?" I asked him.

"I'm bored," he justified.

"What are you talking about?" I countered. "You've got one of the best teachers I know, you're learning about Joseph Smith, and you're studying the Doctrine and Covenants. How can you be bored?"

"Well, okay," he admitted. "It's not all that bad. I just don't want to learn what he's teaching right now."

"All right," I said. "And what *do* you want to learn?"

He was straightforward. "I want to learn about Satan."

So, starting that afternoon, he and I opened the scriptures and began to learn about Satan. For the next two days, I'd pull him from class and we'd spend sixth hour reading scriptures about the origin and nature of the adversary—all without recourse to ghost stories or Ouija boards.

After three days, I waited in my office for him at the appointed hour and he didn't come. I found him in his assigned seat in seminary, behaving and ready to be a traditional student again.

"So," I observed, "after three days of *me,* I see you're ready to go back to class."

"Oh, no," he said quickly. "It's not that. I enjoyed the stuff we talked about, and I'm grateful for your time. It's not you." And then he answered soberly, "It's Satan. I'm sick of him. I don't want to waste my time on him any longer."

In our every contact with Satan, he tends to wear out his welcome quickly, particularly to those with any portion of the Spirit. This book could easily be a thick and ponderous volume. (After all, Satan has a long and sordid career, complete with dark documentation.) But after due consideration, I realized that a brief exposé on the adversary was about as much as any of us could endure in one swallow. That is probably true because Satan's activities are so completely contrary to our progress. No acquaintance with the devil can exalt any of us.

In one of his final First Presidency messages, President James E. Faust offered some critical counsel as he prefaced his remarks on the adversary:

> I approach this [topic] prayerfully, because Satan is not an enlightening subject. . . .
>
> It is not good practice to become intrigued by Satan and his mysteries. No good can come from getting close to evil. Like playing with fire, it is too easy to get burned.[1]

Indeed, any study of the adversary should focus on the contrasts between the prince of darkness and the Prince of Peace, the Light of the World—together with a clear recognition and a resounding declaration that each of us is saved only through the grace of God and the Atonement of Jesus Christ.

The only justification for giving any studious attention to the enemies of God is to enable us to better withstand them. As a matter of fact, it's dangerous not to have a basic awareness of the powers of evil. Understanding the difference between the darkness and the light is critical.

President Brigham Young taught,

> I will tell you a truth. . . neither you nor I would ever be prepared to be crowned in the celestial kingdom of our Father and our God, without devils in this world. . . . We are obliged to know and understand them, one as well as the other, in order to prepare us for the day that is coming, and for our exaltation. . . . *We must know the evil in order to know the good.*[2]

That understanding carries with it a caution that the knowledge and power of Satan are nothing to be trifled with.

President Young made that warning very clear:

> People are liable in many ways to be led astray by the power of the adversary, for they do not fully understand that it is a hard matter for them to always distinguish the things of God from the things of the devil. There is but one way by which they can know the difference, and that is by the light of the spirit of revelation, even the spirit of our Lord Jesus Christ. Without this we are all liable to be led astray.[3]

I pray that the Spirit may accompany us as we study the nature and the reality of Satan, with an understanding that the references we will examine from the scriptures and from modern prophets are not mere intellectual calisthenics. We undertake this study with an eye of preparation and a voice of warning, as the Apostle Paul teaches,

> Lest Satan should get an advantage of us: for we are not ignorant of his devices. (2 Corinthians 2:11)

## • Notes

1. James E. Faust, "The Forces That Will Save Us." *Ensign*, Jan. 2007, 5.

2. Brigham Young, in *Journal of Discourses* (London: Latter-day Saints' Book Depot, 1854–86), 4:373. (Italics added.)

3. Brigham Young, in *Journal of Discourses*, 3:43.

# 1

# THE GOD OF THIS WORLD

As a kid, my favorite TV show was *The Twilight Zone*. In the 1960s, *The Twilight Zone* was the premiere fantasy/sci-fi program of its day. Every Friday night the show presented television-viewing America with a half-hour morality play disguised as good, old-fashioned, black-and-white horror. For me and my boyhood pals, it was the week's greatest thirty minutes of entertainment.

In the series's second season, *The Twilight Zone*'s creator, Rod Serling, hosted an episode that served as an ideal introduction to the machinations of the adversary. The story, entitled "The Howling Man," became one of the classic installments of the long-running series.

In the tale, a traveler in post–World War I Europe chances upon an old hermitage where a group of eccentric monks hold a young man in a prison cell, claiming that their captive is Satan himself. The prisoner—by all appearances, an innocent victim of religious fanaticism—pleads with the visiting traveler to help him escape from captivity. In the climax of the story, the traveler decides to risk his life to set the young man free.

Moving stealthily past the sleeping guard in the dead of night, the traveler carefully removes the shepherd's crook that bars the door of the prisoner's cell and opens it wide. But as he does so, the fair-faced innocence of the former captive hardens into a cruel grin. Pitiless and ungrateful, he strikes his rescuer to the ground with a wave of his hand.

The paralyzed traveler watches helplessly as the betrayer strokes his beard, ponders his freedom, and then walks the length of the hall, gradually transforming himself into the prince of darkness. Stopping at the window, he turns and, with one final, malicious glance, vanishes with a flash of smoke into the stormy night.

The traveler collapses to the floor as the brothers of the hermit-age arrive to care for him and to survey, with regret, the escape of the demonic captive.

"I am sorry for you, my son," a white-bearded priest consoles him. "All your life you will remember this night. And you'll know . . . whom you have turned loose upon the world."

"I didn't believe you," the traveler grieves. "I saw him, but I didn't recognize him."

"That is man's weakness," says the old cleric, "and Satan's strength."[1]

## The Fingerprints of Satan

Like I said—classic, psychological suspense/thriller with a touch of the macabre. As kids, we loved it—never suspecting for a minute that we were being taught profound principles of good and evil. And that Friday night I learned a lesson that made an impression on my spongy, preadolescent mind for years to come. For indeed, *that we do not recognize him is man's weakness, and Satan's strength.* In fact, one of Satan's favorite tactics is to convince a naïve world that he doesn't exist at all—that any hype concerning him is mere myth, yellow journalism from the religious paparazzi.

> And behold, others he flattereth away, and telleth them there is no hell; and he saith unto them: *I am no devil, for there is none*—and thus he whispereth in their ears, until he grasps them with his awful chains, from whence there is no deliverance. (2 Nephi 28:22; italics added)

Our response to this decoy was best expressed by one of my old university instructors, the legendary Ivan J. Barrett.

Two protestant churches occupied opposite corners of a small town intersection. Each church had a marquee that was employed to promote their pastor's weekly discourse. One week, the first marquee advertised the title of the upcoming Sunday sermon. It read, "There Ain't No Hell." The next day the second church displayed its message in reply. It read, "The Hell There Ain't."[2] (Pardon me. That's a direct quote.)

The Apostle Paul expressed the principle of Satan's reality in another way.

> For we wrestle not against flesh and blood, but against principalities, against powers, against the rulers of the darkness of this world, against spiritual wickedness in high places. (Ephesians 6:12)

As we adjust our vision, observe closely, and peer past the camouflage, it becomes easy to see that *worldly powers* and the *rulers of darkness* and *spiritual wickedness in high places* have Satan's fingerprints all over them! The key is to acknowledge his active reality and recognize his operations. Satan is the genuine article. He is real—and pure evil.

In this sense, the reality of Satan was, perhaps, the first revelatory lesson of this dispensation. In a pattern that seems consistent in the lives of the prophets, Satan's effort to destroy Joseph Smith was the first response to the boy's prayer in the Sacred Grove.

> I had scarcely [begun to pray], when immediately I was seized upon by some power which entirely overcame me, and had such an astonishing influence over me as to bind my tongue so that I could not speak. Thick darkness gathered around me, and it seemed to me for a time as if I were doomed to sudden destruction.
>
> But, exerting all my powers to call upon God to deliver me out of the power of this enemy which had seized upon me, and at the very moment when I was ready to sink into despair and abandon myself to destruction—not to an imaginary ruin, but to the power of some actual being from the unseen world, who had such marvelous power as I had never before felt in any being—just at this moment of great alarm, I saw a pillar of light exactly over my head. (Joseph Smith—History 1:15–16)

What a terrifying experience for young Joseph—to kneel in prayer to the King of the Universe and receive instead a visit from the prince of darkness. As the scriptural record bears out, Satan typically introduces himself in this fashion: simultaneously with the opening of the windows of heaven. In almost every dispensation of the gospel, whenever the celestial veil has been parted to make it possible for God to communicate with man, Lucifer has been present, ready to disclose a revelation of his own. It is the ultimate dirty trick—one that Satan loves to pull.

The experience of the boy Joseph in the Sacred Grove is our most familiar example, but it is by no means isolated. It was so with Satan's primordial appearance on earth in the Garden of Eden, immediately following the account of creation.

> And Satan put it into the heart of the serpent, . . . and he sought also to beguile Eve, . . . wherefore he sought to destroy the world. (Moses 4:6)

Lucifer certainly doesn't waste any time. He took unfair advantage of the innocence of Adam and Eve. (But, as we know, it all worked out.)

Satan was also there in the lone and dreary world when the plan of salvation was presented to Adam's children.

> And Adam and Eve blessed the name of God, and they made all things known unto their sons and their daughters. (Moses 5:12)

Adam and Eve were good parents. Most of us today have good parents. But as in the first days of history, good parents alone are not enough. A willing generation must be ready to follow. That up-and-coming generation has always been fertile ground for Satan's seeds of deception.

> And Satan came among them, saying: I am also a son of God; and he commanded them, saying: Believe it not; and they believed it not, and they loved Satan more than God. (Moses 5:13)

Foolish kids! All of us are such foolish kids. In any age, at any age, many of us allow ourselves to be deceived. But Satan particularly considers the youth of the world to be an easy mark. We need to make sure that we are not!

Satan was present in Canaan when Abraham made sacrifice in preparation to behold Jehovah, and to receive the cherished covenant.

> And when the sun was going down, a deep sleep fell upon Abram; and, lo, an horror of great darkness [Satan] fell upon him. . .
>
> And it came to pass, that, when the sun went down, and it was dark, behold a smoking furnace, and a burning lamp [the presence of the Lord] that passed between those pieces.
>
> In the same day the Lord made a covenant with Abram. (Genesis 15:12, 17–18)

If we read the scriptures carefully, we begin to discover Satan, cloaked in disguise, manifesting himself everywhere.

He appeared to Moses when that prophet was "caught up into an exceedingly high mountain" (Moses 1:1).

> And the presence of God withdrew from Moses, that his glory was not upon Moses. . . . And as he was left unto himself, he fell unto the earth.
>
> And it came to pass that it was for the space of many hours before Moses did again receive his natural strength like unto man. . . .
>
> And it came to pass that . . . Satan came tempting him, saying: Moses, son of man, worship me. (Moses 1:9–10, 12)

Not even Christ was exempt from Satan's efforts. In the meridian of time he made his appearance at a pivotal point in the Savior's life—*after* His baptism and *before* His ministry.

> Then was Jesus led up of the Spirit into the wilderness to be tempted of the devil. [Note the correction of the Joseph Smith Translation, "to be with God."]
>
> And when he had fasted forty days and forty nights, he was afterward an hungred.
>
> And when the tempter came to him, he said, If thou be the Son of God, command that these stones be made bread. (Matthew 4:1–3)

We perceive several truths from these examples. But one of the simplest and yet most important lessons we learn is that our Heavenly Father is not a meddling, interfering, overprotective parent. Oh, he's always there and always willing to answer our calls of distress in one form or another, but he knows that there are some things we need to learn through experience. Through confrontations such as these, our Heavenly Father has allowed his children to learn their foundational lesson of theology—the truth that there are two powers in the universe. One leads to truth; the other to falsehood. One exists to exalt man; the other to destroy him. One represents a loving, personal God; the other a malevolent, personal devil.

Each of us has to go through that tutorial in one form or another. The lesson is not an easy one, particularly when dealing with a master of disguise. Just ask Adam, Eve, Abraham, Moses, Joseph Smith, or Jesus Christ.

The Apostle Paul spoke of this devious deception in the early Christian Church:

For such are false apostles, deceitful workers, transforming themselves into the apostles of Christ.

And no marvel; *for Satan himself is transformed into an angel of light.* (2 Corinthians 11:13–14; italics added)

Regarding this masquerade, Brigham Young stated,

If true principles are revealed from heaven to men, and if there are angels, and there is a possibility of their communicating to the human family, always look for an opposite power, an evil power, to give manifestations also; look out for the counterfeit.[3]

President Joseph F. Smith made this observation of how skilled Satan can be in his pretense.

We have been deceived; we thought that the devil had long horns and tail, a cloven foot, and was black, hideous, and grinning; but when we find him out he is a gentlemen in black broad cloth, with a smooth tongue, pleasant countenance, high forehead, and . . . quite a good looking fellow.[4]

The First Presidency in 1942 described the complete impersonation of the great pretender.

He is working under such perfect disguise that many do not recognize either him or his methods. There is no crime he would not commit, no debauchery he would not set up, no plague he would not send, no heart that he would not break, no life he would not take, no soul he would not destroy. He comes as a thief in the night; he is a wolf in sheep's clothing.[5]

Joseph Smith, who learned to recognize the adversary through hard experience, described Satan's method in perfect simplicity.

It is that smooth, sophisticated influence of the devil, by which he deceives the whole world.[6]

# Gifts of the "Spirit"

The Prophet Joseph Smith made it clear that this challenge from the dark side is not unique to our time, culture, or dispensation.

It is evident from the Apostles' writings, that many false spirits existed in their day, and had "gone forth into the world," and that it needed intelligence which God alone could impart to detect false spirits, and to prove what spirits were of God. The world in general [has] been grossly ignorant in regard to this one thing, and why should they be otherwise—for "the things of God knoweth no man, but the Spirit of God."[7]

So, the Holy Ghost is the key to recognizing the difference between evil spirits and good spirits. This is particularly true when dealing with manifestations that we *associate* with the Holy Ghost. You see, some spiritual experiences are good and some are bad. Again Joseph Smith taught,

One great evil is, that men are ignorant of the nature of spirits; their power, laws, government, intelligence, etc., and imagine that when there is anything like power, revelation, or vision manifested, that it must be of God.[8]

The standoff between Moses and the magicians of Pharaoh's court illustrates this contrast of miraculous powers. It was an awesome display.

And Moses and Aaron went in unto Pharaoh, and they did so as the Lord had commanded: and Aaron cast down his rod before Pharaoh, and before his servants, and *it became a serpent.* (Exodus 7:10; italics added)

Very impressive. But Pharaoh was not to be outdone.

Then Pharaoh also called the wise men and the sorcerers: now the magicians of Egypt, they also did in like manner with their enchantments.
     For they cast down every man his rod, *and they became serpents.* (Exodus 7:11–12; italics added)

Now, we wonder if Moses anticipated this development. Pharaoh's response to Moses's miracle was very "ho hum." "Moses performs magic. Fine!" he muses. "Well, my sorcerers can perform magic too." However, in the face of Satan's "signs and wonders," the Lord *did* want to make a point.

*But Aaron's rod swallowed up their rods.* (Exodus 7:12; italics added)

That should have been the end of it. The point should have been made. But for prideful, faithless Pharaoh, this only meant that Moses shopped at a better magic store. Egypt's ruler was unable to recognize the real power of God because he was so focused on the counterfeit. Thus blinded, he refused to free the children of Israel—until the signs and plagues from God became extremely painful. But that is another story.

This experience teaches us that Satan indeed has power; but the lesson to remember is that the power of God will always predominate in this uneven matchup. And it is critical for us to be able to discern between the two. Satan and his followers continue to manufacture imitation miracles in every age. Therefore, the gift of tongues, visions, dreams, prophecy, and so forth, should always be considered gifts of the Spirit. The challenge is to determine *which* spirit.

To make that statement is not to imply that all such manifestations outside the Church are from Satan. However, the prophets and the scriptures do teach us to "try the spirits" (1 John 4:1). Divine revelation provides us with valuable measures that teach us how to make such an evaluation—based on appropriateness and the established order in the kingdom of God.

The Prophet Joseph counseled,

> Not every spirit, or vision, or singing, is of God. . . . Speak not in the gift of tongues without understanding it, or without interpretation. The devil can speak in tongues; . . . [he] can speak in English or Dutch. Let no one speak in tongues unless he [can] interpret, except by the consent of the one who is placed to preside.[9]

The early Saints were also acquainted with dramatic demonstrations such as swooning, jumping, shouting, or even fainting which occurred in churches of the day. These emotional displays were often attributed to the Spirit. And believe me, they could present quite a spectacle. With regard to any such manifestation, the Prophet questioned,

> A manifestation of what? Is there any intelligence communicated? Are the curtains of heaven withdrawn, or the purposes of God developed? . . . All the intelligence that can be obtained from them when they arise, is a shout of "glory," or "hallelujah," or some incoherent expression.[10]

The world then is full of spiritual exhibitions. We need to consider their source. Joseph concluded,

> Is God the author of all this? If not of all of it, which does He recognize? Surely, such a heterogeneous mass of confusion never can enter into the kingdom of heaven.[11]

## Unmasking the Deceiver

What enabled our greatest scriptural heroes to vanquish the adversary was ultimately the strength of their personal righteousness and the power of the priesthood. But initially their first defense was the spiritual discernment to identify Satan as an imposter.

The Prophet Joseph Smith taught,

> A man must have the discerning of spirits before he can drag into daylight this hellish influence and unfold it unto the world in all its soul-destroying, diabolical, and horrid colors; for nothing is a greater injury to the children of men than to be under the influence of a false spirit when they think they have the Spirit of God.[12]

On more than one occasion, Brother Joseph provided the keys to distinguish between a false spirit and a true messenger. One such key was as simple as paying attention to detail.

> There have also been ministering angels in the Church which were of Satan appearing as an angel of light. A sister in the state of New York had a vision, . . . and saw a glorious personage descending, arrayed in white, with sandy colored hair.[13]

This "angel" told her, among other things, that her husband had been called to do great things, but that he must not go more than one hundred miles from home, threatening a vague destruction if he exceeded the travel limit. This was inconvenient since God had called the husband to go to the ends of the earth. (Satan will go to great lengths to misdirect us from our foreordained missions.)

Well, the false spirit was detected and the husband served his mission, going more than a thousand miles, without the fulfillment of the foretold catastrophe. The Prophet concludes,

> How, it may be asked, was this known to be a bad angel? By the color of his hair; that is one of the signs that he can be known by, and by his contradicting a former revelation.[14]

Another test, included in the Doctrine and Covenants, involved a performance of the most commonplace of greetings. After all, if a supernatural visitor appears to us—be it angel or demon—the least we can do is be polite.

When a messenger comes saying he has a message from God, offer him your hand and request him to shake hands with you.

And if he be an angel [a resurrected personage] he will do so, and you will feel his hand.

If he be the spirit of a just man made perfect [not resurrected] he will come in his glory; for that is the only way he can appear—

Ask him to shake hands with you, but he will not move, because it is contrary to the order of heaven for a just man to deceive; but he will still deliver his message.

If it be the devil as an angel of light, when you ask him to shake hands he will offer you his hand, and you will not feel anything; you may therefore detect him. (D&C 129:4–8)

But none of these tests of authenticity are as practical to you and me as the simple measure of listening to our heart. How we "feel" is of the utmost importance in discerning good from evil.

*And that which doth not edify is not of God, and is darkness.*
*That which is of God is light. . . .*
And again, verily I say unto you, . . . that you may know the truth, that you may chase darkness from among you. (D&C 50:23–25; italics added)

Darkness depresses, discourages, and tears us down. Light not only dispels the darkness, but edifies, enriches, and lifts us up. This light is universally good.

*For the word of the Lord is truth, and whatsoever is truth is light, and whatsoever is light is Spirit, even the Spirit of Jesus Christ.*
And the Spirit giveth light to every man that cometh into the world; and the Spirit enlighteneth every man through the world, that hearkeneth to the voice of the Spirit. (D&C 84:45–46; italics added)

Light, truth, intelligence—all are synonymous with this Spirit which speaks to our heart and drives away evil.

For behold, the Spirit of Christ is given to every man, that he may know good from evil; wherefore, I show unto you the way to judge; *for every thing which inviteth to do good, and to persuade to believe in Christ, is sent forth by the power and the gift of Christ; wherefore ye may know with a perfect knowledge it is of God.*

*But whatsoever thing persuadeth men to do evil, and believe not in Christ, and deny him, and serve not God, then ye may know with a perfect*

*knowledge it is of the devil;* for after this manner doth the devil work, for
he persuadeth no man to do good, no, not one; neither do his angels;
neither do they who subject themselves unto him. (Moroni 7:16–17;
italics added)

In early 1844, Charles Lambert, a dedicated convert from England, arrived in Nauvoo, anxious to apply his skills as a master craftsman to the construction of the rising temple. However, there was no
money to pay him, and as he worked, his family began to want for
the essentials of life. Still, Brother Lambert continued to labor on the
Lord's house until the financial strain became almost unbearable.

Under these circumstances he was walking home from the temple
one day when he met a well-dressed stranger who stopped him on the
street.

"Is your name Charles Lambert?" the stranger inquired.

"It is," answered Lambert.

"Well, then," continued the stranger with a smile, "my name is
Higgins and my home is in Missouri. I have heard of your skill as a
workman and I want you to go up to Missouri and work for me. You
are not appreciated or properly paid here. If you will quit the temple
and come to work for me, you can name your own price and you will
be sure of your pay. You see, I have plenty of money with which to pay
you."

Thrusting his hand into his pocket, he drew out his fist, full of
ten-and twenty-dollar gold pieces, which he displayed in a tempting
manner.

"Accept my offer," coaxed Higgins, "and submit no longer to the
unfair treatment you receive at the temple."

Lambert was annoyed at the suggestion that the Church would
wrong him but still wished to be polite. "I thank you for your offer,"
he replied, "but I could not think of accepting it. You see I have no
complaint to make of my treatment at the temple, and the price you
would pay me for work elsewhere will not influence me in the matter.
I intend to continue on at the temple on principle."

Lambert nodded his head cordially. "I thank you again, and good-
day."

Then, walking past the stranger, Lambert continued down the
street. But almost immediately the question occurred to him as to how

the stranger knew his name or learned of his skill as a craftsman. He
turned back to the stranger to inquire of him,[15]

> When lo, he was nowhere to be seen. He had disappeared as completely
> as if the ground had opened and swallowed him, . . .
>
> [Charles Lambert's] opinion then was, and remained so up to the
> day of his death, that he had been talking with no other than Satan, the
> prince of tempters, and though he had not yielded to his tempting offer,
> he was vexed with himself for listening to him at all.[16]

That Satan is real, that he is inexorably evil, that he is a master of
deception, and that he may be distinguished from beings of light are
first among the vital lessons in the historical School of the Prophets.
To understand this fact is critical in order to recognize Satan and
defeat him.

# Notes

1. Charles Beaumont and Rod Serling, "The Howling Man," *The Twilight Zone,* season 2, episode 5, directed by Douglas Heyes, aired November 4, 1960 (Beverly Hills, CA: Cayuga Productions, 1964), DVD.

2. Ivan J. Barrett, in lecture notes taken by author, Brigham Young University, December, 1970.

3. Brigham Young, in *Journal of Discourses* (London: Latter-day Saints' Book Depot, 1854–86), 7:240.

4. Joseph F. Smith, in *Journal of Discourses*, 11:313.

5. James R. Clark, comp., *Messages of the First Presidency of The Church of Jesus Christ of Latter-day Saints* (Salt Lake City: Bookcraft, 1965–75), 6:179.

6. Joseph Smith, *Teachings of the Prophet Joseph Smith*, comp. Joseph Fielding Smith (Salt Lake City: Deseret Book, 1938), 270.

7. Ibid., 202.

8. Ibid., 203.

9. Ibid., 162.

10. Ibid., 204.

11. Ibid.

12. Ibid., 205.

13. Ibid., 214–15.

14. Ibid.

15. Alma P. Burton and Clea M. Burton, *Stories from Mormon History* (Salt Lake City: Deseret Book, 1960), 221–23.

16. Ibid., 223.

# 2

# THE PREMORTAL SON OF THE MORNING

In his own right, Satan is a celebrity—albeit a demented one. Superstar of art, literature, and popular entertainment, his claim to fame here on earth is undisputed. Consider the paintings and sculptures in which he is the central figure—or at least has played a feature role. He and his minions pepper the walls and ceiling of the Sistine Chapel. Think about the central parts he's taken in classic poetry, such as *Paradise Lost* or Dante's *Inferno*, not to mention his feature roles in some of the worst modern pulp fiction ever written. And who can debate his critical influence in motion pictures?

Darth Vader and the dark side of the Force were the only elements that made the Star Wars saga really interesting. Sauron and the power he wielded was the ultimate threat to all Middle-earth in *The Lord of the Rings*. And the entire Harry Potter series would have been very dull without Voldemort—(sorry) "He Who Must Not Be Named."

Well, Satan may serve well for medieval art, masterpieces of literature, and 3-D cinema bursting with special effects, but the truth is, life on earth would be quite pleasant without him—necessary though he may be to this probationary estate.

Of course, Satan's participation in our lives began long before mortality. And any understanding of his origin requires us to go beyond the veil, into the timeless realm of premortal life.

## Rebellion at the Grand Council

The prophet Moses gives us our first glimpse of Satan, in what we might call his spiritual adolescence.

> That Satan . . . is the same which was from the beginning, and he came
> before me, saying—Behold, here am *I*, send *me*, *I* will be thy son, and
> *I* will redeem all mankind, that one soul shall not be lost, and surely
> *I* will do it; wherefore give *me* thine honor. (Moses 4:1; italics added)

This is our introduction to Lucifer—already a dangerous egomaniac. He is unbelievable! Everything is *I, I, me, me,* and ultimately, *mine.* And while it is an informative first impression, it is followed immediately by an even more revealing introduction—to an individual whose reply to the Father sets him apart as the hero of our story.

> But, behold, my Beloved Son, which was my Beloved and Chosen from
> the beginning, said unto me—Father, *thy* will be done, and the glory
> be *thine* forever. (Moses 4:2; italics added)

Now there is a contrast! And I hope we are all sensitive to it. In Lucifer's case, it was all about him—totally self directed. *I, me, mine.* But when Jehovah responded, *he* was not the issue. All that mattered to him was the will and glory of the Father. Lucifer and Jehovah, as we first meet both of them in the premortal world, are 180-degree opposites—literally poles apart. That difference made *all* the difference.

> Wherefore, because that Satan rebelled against me, and sought to
> destroy the agency of man, which I, the Lord God, had given him, and
> also, that I should give unto him mine own power; by the power of
> mine Only Begotten, I caused that he should be cast down;
> *And he became Satan, yea, even the devil, the father of all lies, to
> deceive and to blind men, and to lead them captive at his will, even as
> many as would not hearken unto my voice.* (Moses 4: 3–4; italics added)

Abraham gives us a similar, if abbreviated, account.

> And the Lord said: Whom shall I send? And one answered like unto the
> Son of Man: Here am I, send me. And another answered and said: Here
> am I, send me. And the Lord said: I will send the first.
> And the second was angry, and kept not his first estate; and at that
> day, many followed after him. (Abraham 3:27–28)

These few verses of modern revelation teach volumes regarding Satan—matters of which the rest of the world is ignorant: that Satan was in the beginning with the rest of us in premortal life, that he was a preeminent personality there, and that we knew him well.

Joseph Smith, in the Doctrine and Covenants, spoke of Lucifer's standing in those realms of glory.

> And this we saw also, and bear record, that an angel of God who was in authority in the presence of God, who rebelled against the Only Begotten Son whom the Father loved and who was in the bosom of the Father, was thrust down from the presence of God and the Son. (D&C 76:25)

Lucifer was an honored and influential person in premortality. He was an angel of God, as well as our friend and brother. Think about it. There was a time when we knew him, saw him regularly and, no doubt, interacted with him. And he fell. That this event was devastating to us is indicated by the next verse.

> And was called Perdition, for the heavens wept over him—he was Lucifer, a son of the morning.
>     And we beheld, and lo, he is fallen! is fallen, even a son of the morning! (D&C 76:26–27)

Thus is recorded the downfall of Lucifer, an individual of authority in the presence of God, whose very name means "bearer of light." Little wonder the heavens shook and we wept over him. That he, of all spirits, had turned to the darkness literally broke our hearts.

> For we beheld Satan, that old serpent, even the devil, who rebelled against God, and sought to take the kingdom of our God and his Christ. (D&C 76:28)

The scriptures explain that Lucifer was "thrust down" (D&C 76:25). But that oversimplifies the issue, as if the poor boy were sent to bed without his supper for misbehaving. Abraham's short recital of the conflict in heaven describes what happened more realistically.

> And the second *was angry*, and *kept not* his first estate. (Abraham 3:28; italics added)

This consequence was not *really* the Father's doing. It was still all about Lucifer. Like all the trouble we get ourselves into when we disobey, Lucifer's punishment was completely under his control. He got angry (a stupid weakness) and "kept not" his first estate. It was his decision.

With regard to Satan's offenses, the scriptures are very specific.

> Wherefore, because that [1] *Satan rebelled against me*, and [2] *sought to destroy the agency of man*, which I, the Lord God, had given him, and also, [3] *that I should give unto him mine own power*; by the power of mine Only Begotten, I caused that he should be cast down. (Moses 4:3; italics added)

## First

### "Satan Rebelled Against Me"

We probably all agree that rebelling against God would be a bad idea. It makes us wonder why we all, so foolishly, do it. This rebellion is the simplest definition of sin, which Lucifer committed with his free will. What made Lucifer's sin so serious was his *full knowledge* in committing it.

Elder John A. Widtsoe expressed it this way,

> The serious consequences of disobeying the truth are clearly stated in a revelation given to the Prophet Joseph Smith: "There are many who have been ordained among you, whom I have called, but few of them are chosen. They who are not chosen have sinned a very grievous sin, in that they are walking in darkness at noon-day." (Doctrine and Covenants 95:5–6)
>
> That is the sin of sins: To walk with closed eyes in the midst of light; to know truth, yet not to yield to it. *That sin threw the Son of the Morning from his high pedestal in the divine council into the depth of evil, and made him Satan, the teacher and defender of untruth.*[1]

## Second

### "Satan Sought to Destroy the Agency of Man"

This, of course, is the "meat and potatoes" of Lucifer's transgression. The traditional Latter-day Saint interpretation of this crime is that Lucifer attempted to deprive mankind of free will in mortality.

In the words of Elder Joseph Fielding Smith,

> It was Satan's plan to destroy [our] agency and force men to do his will.[2]

This was also taught by Elder James E. Talmage:

His selfish ambition led him to aspire to the glory and power of the Father, to secure which he made the pernicious proposition to redeem the human family by compulsion.[3]

However, there are inherent problems with this "tyranny of righteousness" proposition—the greatest being that Lucifer's devoted followers would never have smiled favorably on any proposal that would have *forced* them to obey all the commandments in order to qualify for exaltation.

Not only would it never have worked, but if we understand the nature of the rebellious third part, we could not imagine their being enthusiastic about such a plan or that they would be willing to wage war to impose it. After all, none of us like being told what to do. As teenagers, we are all especially resistant to any set of circumstances under which we are compelled to do anything. But we are especially rebellious about being forced to choose righteously. "I'm sixteen and my parents still *make* me go to church! Why don't they let me use my *free agency*!" (Not a scriptural term, incidentally.) Sound familiar? Why would we suppose that Satan's premortal followers would feel differently?

Even our official seminary curriculum acknowledges,

Most people think that he [Lucifer] would have forced us to do right, but *that is only one possibility.*[4]

We learn from the second chapter of 2 Nephi that agency actually requires four conditions to be in operation. These conditions are the following:

The Power to Choose
Alternative Choices
Knowledge of Good and Evil
Law

Let's take a moment and consider each condition carefully.

*(1) The Power to Choose*

Wherefore, the Lord God gave unto man that he should act for himself. (2 Nephi 2:16)

This element of agency seems obvious and elementary, but it is fundamental. We must be able to choose. Let's suppose that salvation in some alternate universe requires us to consume large quantities of ice cream. (What a delightful world!) It would be logical to assume that this universe would not only have to have an ice cream store, but that it be open for business 24/7. If not, there would be no agency. We need to be able to make the choice at any time!

## (2) Alternative Choices

> For it must needs be, that there is an opposition in all things.
> (2 Nephi 2:11)

Agency also requires alternate selections between good and evil—offering us a *real* choice. Let's imagine our ice cream store again. It's open round the clock now, but the only flavor available is chocolate. That may not seem like a problem to some people. But the reality is that you can't really choose if you don't have another choice—no matter how much you like chocolate.

Henry Ford, whose standardized automobiles dominated the American marketplace at the turn of the twentieth century, said of his Model T Ford, "You can buy a car in any color you want . . . so long as it's black."[5] There is no such thing as agency without choices.

## (3) Knowledge of Good and Evil

> And because that they are redeemed from the fall they have become free forever, knowing good from evil. (2 Nephi 2:26)

We need a clear understanding between the choices offered us—right and wrong, salvation or damnation.

Even if our ice cream store has been restocked with all thirty-one flavors listed in the official ice cream lexicon, this variety of choices would be academic unless it were made clear to us that vanilla *is* the flavor that we need to eat in order to earn a place in the celestial kingdom. We need to know which is which for agency to properly operate.

And finally agency requires one more thing.

## (4) Law

> They have become free forever, . . . to act for themselves and not to be acted upon, save it be by the punishment of the law . . . according to the commandments which God hath given. (2 Nephi 2:26)

Law imposes order and defines which choices are correct—that there is indeed a *right* choice. And that right choice (at our hypothetical ice cream store) is vanilla. However, in real life as well as eternity, the right choices established by law are not arbitrary or capricious. The laws set the standard, and there is a reason they do. In school, for example, the elimination of grading standards would award every student with an A+, even those who were failing. This might seem nice in an "everybody's a winner" society. But the new, nonstandard policy wouldn't prepare anyone for life or be fair to those who *did* earn As.

The laws of the universe are even more important. Unlike the rules of a game or a grading policy, the commandments are set in stone, like the laws of motion or physics. They are what they are and what they have always been. They cannot be changed arbitrarily or discarded by majority vote. They determine the pathway to exaltation and cannot be altered. Law is the foundation of agency.

So, in seeking "to destroy the agency of man," Lucifer might have considered the removal of one, or a combination of any of these four components of agency.

Denying us the *power to choose* has been our most traditional interpretation of Satan's plan, as suggested by Elder Smith and Elder Talmage. (You will eat the ice cream I tell you to eat!)

Satan also might have attempted to remove the element of *alternative choices—opposition.* (You can have any flavor you want as long as it's vanilla.) This is conceivable in terms of ice cream, but difficult if not impossible to structure a world in which the *only* choices available were the correct ones.

He could also have restricted the *knowledge of good and evil.* (There is no flavor in existence except vanilla. Trust me!) This has been a favorite technique of earthly tyrants in totalitarian societies—and ultimately it never works.

However, several modern prophets have suggested that Lucifer's "plan" contemplated the elimination of *law.* (All right, everybody, it's party time—all you can eat of any flavor you want. And pay no attention to that gnawing feeling of indigestion.) This proposal would have ignored the actual requirements for exaltation, pretending that the laws of the universe did not exist. It would have qualified us for nothing. But from Satan's point of view, this scheme would have been the simplest answer to meet his self-centered objectives.

Like the class where everyone gets an A, a purposeful lowering of the bar would provide effort-free salvation to even the most mediocre of Satan's vast army of underachieving minions. It is easy to understand why a third part of the hosts of heaven would be enthusiastic about a promise of exaltation that required no effort or sacrifice. Lucifer's plan was the equivalent of "Salvation Made Easy." It was the ultimate entitlement.

Consider this statement of President J. Reuben Clark:

> As I read the scriptures, Satan's plan required one of two things: Either compulsion of the mind, the spirit, the intelligence of man, *or else saving men in sin*. I question whether the intelligence of man can be compelled. Certainly men cannot be saved in sin, because the laws of salvation and exaltation are founded in righteousness, not in sin.[6]

However, "saving men in sin" seems to have been precisely what Lucifer proposed to the hosts of heaven.

Elder John A. Widtsoe also taught this interpretation:

> In the heavens, in a great council, the plans for preexistent man's descent to earth were discussed. The right of free agency proposed by God, the Father of us all, became the issue. A foremost son of God, Lucifer, . . . undertook to destroy this mark of eternal, intelligent man. He proposed that man should not be subject to the trials and tribulations, the sins and sorrows, accompanying striving man as a free agent. Instead, he proposed that the waiting spirits would be placed on earth, in beautiful surroundings, with never a care or sorrow. Everything would be provided. It would be a regimented, supervised, guarded and guaranteed excursion—everything first class. In course of time they would be returned to their spiritual abode, bloated and dull.[7]

Sounds pretty good (except for that "bloated and dull" part) until you realize that Lucifer's plan would have left nothing for man to do. Bored and inactive, we would have atrophied into unproductive, spiritual drones. We would have developed neither the intelligence nor the proficiency to qualify ourselves for celestial rewards—if eternal life would have even been tolerable to us under those conditions.

Elder Bruce R. McConkie expressed the same eternal principles this way:

But Lucifer wanted to abandon the testing or probationary part of mortality; he wanted to take away the agency of man, forestall the need of judgment according to works, and impose salvation upon all men *without effort on their part*—an impossible thing since there can be no progression except by the upward pull of obedience to law.[8]

So, there would be no judgment, since there would be no rules. That also sounds nice on the face of it. However, there would also be no growth, since it is only through obedience to law that we may progress. The son of the morning conveniently ignored this eternal law. No sense letting the facts get in the way of a great idea. And the sluggards of heaven loved Satan's idea.

Elder Orson Pratt described the reaction of Lucifer's enthusiastic groupies:

They hearkened to his proposition; they thought it would be a very great and important thing to destroy the agency of man . . . and to redeem them all *in their sins*, and consequently they joined with this rebellious character; hence came the fallen angels.[9]

You may have noticed that the elimination of law, key to the destruction of agency and the plan of salvation, has been effectively transferred to the earth. Nehor in the Book of Mormon convincingly taught that all men should be saved, regardless of effort:

And he had gone about among the people, preaching to them that which he termed to be the word of God, bearing down against the church; declaring unto the people that every priest and teacher ought to become popular. (Alma 1:3)

An excellent idea . . . especially for Nehor. In his self-centeredness, he is a carbon copy of Satan. But he's not through:

And he also testified unto the people that *all mankind should be saved at the last day*, and that they need not fear nor tremble, but that they might lift up their heads and rejoice; for the Lord had created all men, *and had also redeemed all men; and, in the end, all men should have eternal life*. (Alma 1:4; italics added)

Satan's doctrine doesn't change that much. This philosophy of salvation without the need of Christ was only one step away from the atheistic moral relativism of Korihor:

> And this Anti-Christ . . . began to preach unto the people that there
> should be no Christ. (Alma 30:12)

With that Godless introduction, Korihor's fuzzy logic led him
from one blasphemy to another—including the denial of prophecy,
revelation, and the remission of sin. All of these doctrines he labeled as
"foolish traditions" and "the effect of a frenzied mind" (Alma 30: 14,
16). (Atheism has remained consistently arrogant throughout history.)

> And many more such things did he say unto them, telling them that
> there could be no atonement made for the sins of men, but every man
> fared in this life according to the management of the creature; there-
> fore every man prospered according to his genius, and that every man
> conquered according to his strength; *and whatsoever a man did was no
> crime.* (Alma 30:17; italics added)

The servants of Satan consistently promise us happiness through
the elimination of the law. And to a small, carnal mind the suggestion
makes distorted sense. The "if it feels good" policy does seem to guarantee pleasure and freedom. However, as Moses argued with his people
in Cecil B. DeMille's *The Ten Commandments*, "There is no freedom
without the law."[10] Like the string that holds a kite in the air, the commandments do not inhibit freedom—they guarantee it. Contrary to
the persuasions of Nehor and Korihor, we can't just decide on our own
that the rules—or in our case, the commandments—don't matter. If
we want agency, the commandments matter a great deal.

Both of these religious "progressives" craved the adoration by their
followers which they courted by handing out salvation, free of charge,
under the guise of equality for all, setting a pattern for demagogues
in any age.[11] Both suffered death for the crimes associated with their
apostasy. Both were abandoned by Satan in their hour of need. Both
acknowledged their fault and the demonic source of their deception.

In the case of Korihor, he demanded a sign through the prophet
Alma—and Alma, by the power of the priesthood, obliged him.

> Now when Alma had said these words, Korihor was struck dumb, that
> he could not have utterance, according to the words of Alma. (Alma
> 30:50)

After all the falsehoods that Korihor has taught, this is not only
poetic justice—but also a nice break of peace and quiet. But I digress.

> And now when the chief judge saw this, he put forth his hand and wrote unto Korihor, saying, Art thou convinced of the power of God? . . .
>
> And Korihor put forth his hand and wrote saying: . . . I know that nothing save it were the power of God could bring this upon me; yea, and I always knew that there was a God. (Alma 30:51–52)

Duh! It's hard to be patient with someone as spiritually stupid as Korihor. It's also hard to sympathize with him.

> But behold, the devil hath deceived me; for he appeared unto me in the form of an angel, and said unto me: Go and reclaim this people, for they have gone astray after an unknown God. And he said unto me: There is no God; yea and he taught me that which I should say. And I have taught his words; *and I taught them because they were pleasing unto the carnal mind*; and I taught them, even until I had much success, insomuch that *I verily believed that they were true*; and for this cause *I withstood the truth*, even until *I have brought this great curse upon me.* (Alma 30:53; italics added)

That's a pretty hard-luck sob story. It's easy to see how Satan leads us astray. I suppose we might even actually feel a little sorry for Korihor. Nah!

Reduced to poverty, Korihor spent his remaining days begging from door to door for support, until he was trampled to death by the apostate Zoramites. Well, he *did* have it coming. The story ends with an appropriate summary of Satan's relationship with his followers.

> And thus we see the end of him who perverteth the ways of the Lord; and thus we see that the devil will not support his children at the last day, but doth speedily drag them down to hell. (Alma 30:60)

In the end, neither Nehor nor Korihor were the real problem. They were both mere symptoms of the wickedness and faithlessness of the societies that spawned them, and the spiritual indolence of the throngs who followed them—looking for a free ride to happiness and salvation. Nobody can just give that stuff away.

This principle, taught from the Book of Mormon, is also a regular lesson repeated from the pages of history up to the present. Popular religion and the philosophies of men continue to promise happiness and salvation with minimal qualifications in order to appeal to the masses. To all of this the masses respond enthusiastically. And why shouldn't they? It is the ideal highway to heaven from the church of the devil—one that promises everything and requires nothing.

## Third

"Satan Sought Also that I Should Give unto Him Mine Own Power"

In the words of President J. Reuben Clark,

> All he asked of the Father was that the Father abdicate. . . . [He] was to turn all of his power over to Satan, was to disappear, get out of the picture. . . .
>
> What Satan wanted, quite evidently, was the full possession, ownership, of this creation of spirits that is involved in the peopling of this earth; so he tried to get them by gift, and that being denied, he is following along and trying to get us through commission of sin. If we sin sufficiently we become his subjects.[12]

In essence, Lucifer claimed the power of God as his personal reward. We might easily imagine the son of the morning striding up to the throne of the Almighty to boldly announce, "Excuse me, I believe you're sitting in my chair." Lucifer, fired by a lust for preeminence, is thus characterized by Isaiah:

> I will ascend into heaven, I will exalt my throne above the stars of God: . . . I will be like the Most High. (Isaiah 14:13–14)

That is a powerful ego trip.

## The Satanic Pattern

The warning signs provided by the destructive example of Lucifer are worth reexamining.

> Wherefore, because that [1] Satan rebelled against me, and [2] sought to destroy the agency of man, . . . and also, [3] that I should give unto him mine own power, . . . I caused that he should be cast down. (Moses 4:3)

Rebellion against God, the abuse of sacred agency, and lust for power continue to be the hallmarks of Satan's followers. Those who so choose in this life become his children just as did those who followed him in the premortal world.

Therefore, if a man bringeth forth good works he hearkeneth unto the voice of the good shepherd, and he doth follow him; but whosoever bringeth forth evil works, the same becometh a child of the devil, for he hearkeneth unto his voice, and doth follow him.

And whosoever doeth this must receive his wages of him; therefore, for his wages he receiveth death. (Alma 5:41–42)

We all sin against the light to some degree when we disobey the commandments. We all, at some time, misuse our agency and become a law unto ourselves. And all of us have, at one point or another, foolishly entered Satan's employ with an expectation of payment—fun, gain, or the praise of the world. When we do this we join the ranks of the adversary. And the wages are poor. Most frequently he will pay us in worthless currency, as he did Nehor and Korihor.

However, our Father in Heaven makes every effort to persuade us to return to his loving arms and will welcome us back if we will but come again unto him. And the reward is eternal life.

Swen C. Nielsen, Chief of Security at Brigham Young University, tells of a young man he calls Dick. A high school student in Provo, Dick was a known user and dealer in narcotics who had been under investigation by Nielsen's staff for several years.

At long last, law enforcement agents eventually gathered enough evidence to file a felony complaint against Dick. But before the arrest, Dick surprised Nielsen. He walked into the chief's office and asked for an interview. Nielsen invited Dick to sit down, and after an uncomfortable minute, the young man nervously began to speak. He acknowledged that he had already been to see his bishop and his stake president and had entered the pathway to repentance. Now he wanted to tell Nielsen his story. After reading him his Miranda rights and making his legal obligations clear, the chief invited Dick to proceed.

Dick started with his background—his upbringing in a solid Latter-day Saint family, the quality of his family life, and his activity in all the Church programs. He bore witness "that he had always had a testimony of the truthfulness of the gospel" and "that regardless of what he had ever done he had never doubted that the [Church] was true."[13]

Then, gradually, came the disinterest, the rebellion, the choice of unsavory friends, and the eventual drug abuse, which was not a gradual process. His use of narcotics and his success as a dealer were intense and rapid.

> "So it went for two or three years[," he said]. "I was totally dedicated to the use of drugs myself and [getting] others to use [them] as well. . . .
>
> "It occurred to me that I was in the service of Satan." He said that as he began to think of this, . . . he decided to actually enlist himself in the service of the adversary. . . . [He] testified solemnly that he knew that Satan had blessed him for what he had done; that he gave him "things" that he wanted; [and] that he, in effect, prayed to the adversary for rewards. . . . [He said,] "I had actually engaged myself in the service of the adversary and did everything that I did rationally, with full intent."[14]

It was in the midst of these realizations that Dick attended a rock concert in Salt Lake City. He said that this particular concert was more extreme and demonic than any others he had ever been to, and that he could feel the presence of evil there as almost a tangible power. That evil manifested itself in acts of "orderly confusion" and violence throughout the concert.[15] And the oppressive feeling of evil persisted when the concert was over.

Afterwards he went to a nearby home where he felt the same evil permeating the air. But he didn't feel the true strength of the evil until he reclined on the floor. While in this position he became aware of a power which seemed to exert a physical force against him. It increased in intensity.

He instantly became frightened, and while he was powerless to rise from the floor, "he said a communication came to his mind."[16]

"You have performed well," said the voice. "You have become a candidate for further power—power that will be given to you if you will but do some additional tasks that you have not yet done."

One of the requirements was that he involve himself in acts of sexual perversion. Another was that the time had come to deny his testimony of the gospel. He contemplated these simple requirements and considered the promised rewards. He had already made the choice to serve Satan rather than God, but he had never doubted the truthfulness of the gospel that he was now commanded to deny.

Still lying oppressed on the floor, Dick marshaled all the strength he possessed and loudly declared. "No!"

At that point, the spirit in the residence changed and every occupant departed. He was left alone. In the minutes that followed, the power holding him to the floor dissipated. At length, he struggled to his feet and fled the house.

He explained that the experience had shaken him badly and had made him realize how seriously he needed to change his life. He sought out his priesthood leaders to begin the process of repentance and continued to fight a daily battle in his efforts to pray, clean up his life, and give himself again to Jesus Christ. His life had been filled with sin, and he was haunted over the welfare of his soul. "I don't know if I can ever be forgiven," he confided.

Two years later, after fulfilling the stringent requirements of repentance outlined by both the priesthood and the county attorney, Dick again walked into the office of Swen Nielsen.[17]

> [He] handed [him] a piece of paper and said, "Brother Nielsen, I want you to read this." It was a letter signed by the First Presidency asking him to serve on a mission.[18]

When we rebel against the light, against that which we know to be true, we begin to play a dangerous game that we cannot win. Satan longs to lure us into that trap with promises and words of hollow praise. But the gift of forgiveness is available to every single one of us if we will turn to the Savior, repent, and allow the Atonement to wash us clean.

# NOTES

1. John A. Widtsoe, *An Understandable Religion* (Salt Lake City: Deseret News Press, 1944), 221. (Italics added.)

2. Joseph Fielding Smith, *Answers to Gospel Questions* (Salt Lake City: Deseret Book, 1957) 2:20.

3. James E. Talmage, *Articles of Faith* (Salt Lake City: Deseret News, 1899), 62.

4. Church Educational System, *Old Testament Teacher Resource Manual* (Salt Lake City: Church of Jesus Christ of Latter-day Saints, 1990), 27. (Italics added.)

5. Henry Ford, *My life and Work* (New York City: Doubleday, Page and Co., 1922), 71.

6. J. Reuben Clark, in Conference Report, October 1949, 191–95. (Italics added.)

7. Widtsoe, *An Understandable Religion,* 26.

8. Bruce R. McConkie, "Who Is the Author of the Plan of Salvation?" *The Improvement Era*, May 1953, 323. (Italics added.)

9. Orson Pratt, in *Journal of Discourses* (London: Latter-day Saints' Book Depot, 1854–86), 21:288. (Italics added.)

10. Dorothy Clarke Wilson et al., *The Ten Commandments*, directed by Cecile B. DeMille (1956; Los Angeles, CA: Paramount Pictures, 2013), DVD.

11. Hugh Nibley labels as "liberal" the philosophies of both Nehor and Korihor. See Hugh Nibley, *An Approach to the Book of Mormon* (Salt Lake City: Deseret Book, 1988), 365. Hugh Nibley, *Since Cumorah* (Salt Lake City: Deseret Book, 1988), 380.

12. J. Reuben Clark, in Conference Report, October 1949, 191–95.

13. Margie Calhoun, *When Faith Writes the Story* (Salt Lake City: Bountiful Press, 1993), 220.

14. Ibid., 220–21.

15. Ibid., 221.

16. Ibid.

17. Ibid., 224.

18. Ibid., 219–24.

# 3

# HEAVEN AT WAR

We all know how the drama of the Grand Council played out. God pronounced his decision. After hearing the selfless response of Jehovah contrasted by the narcissistic sophistry of Lucifer, the Father issued the decree: "I will send the first" (Abraham 3:27), thus selecting the Only Begotten to be the "lamb slain from the foundation of the world" (Revelation 13:8).

However, Lucifer was unwilling to accept the Father's will or to accept Jehovah as the Savior and Redeemer. He revolted and became Satan. His course was open, willful rebellion against the Father and the Son, in which he drew a third part of the hosts of heaven after him.

Of the hostilities that followed, we are told few details.

> And there was war in heaven: Michael and his angels fought against the dragon; and the dragon fought and his angels,
>
> And prevailed not; neither was their place found any more in heaven.
>
> And the great dragon was cast out, that old serpent, called the Devil, and Satan, which deceiveth the whole world: he was cast out into the earth, and his angels were cast out with him. (Revelation 12:7–9)

Though the nature of this war has not been made perfectly clear, the conflict seems to have been more than a heated exchange of philosophies—like a protest of college students. The eternal nature of the outcome leaves us with a sense that this was somehow more than just a war of words and ideas—though that was certainly part of it. There were, in a symbolic sense, spiritual hand grenades being lobbed, and spiritual artillery being shot back and forth, as well as spiritual fox holes to take refuge in. It was a real war in a real sense, which culminated in a real victory.

> Now is come salvation, and strength, and the kingdom of our God, and the power of his Christ: for *the accuser of our brethren* is cast down, which *accused them* before our God day and night. (Revelation 12:10; italics added)

If Satan's philosophical attack against the righteous was a barrage of accusations, what form could they have taken? The first probable assault could have easily been a diatribe designed to shake the resolve of those who had accepted the Father's plan of salvation.

We can imagine his shrill denunciation. "You fools! What makes you think the Father's plan can work. It can't! You'll go down to earth and you'll sin. You'll become subject to the law you've so stupidly committed yourselves to and you'll be stranded there, miserable in life and disembodied in death, forever. *You will never return!*"

We learn from Jacob, the brother of Nephi, that this threat was a genuine possibility in which the future devil would, without the intervention of Christ, have played a terrifying part.

> For behold, if the flesh should rise no more our spirits must become subject to that angel who fell from before the presence of the Eternal God, and became the devil, to rise no more.
>
> And our spirits must have become like unto him, and we become devils, angels to a devil, to be shut out from the presence of our God, and to remain with the father of lies, in misery, like unto himself. (2 Nephi 9:8–9)

We can almost picture ourselves listening to Lucifer's threats in premortal life. The possibility of becoming one of the demons of the universe, when our goal had been to become like God, would have been an effective scare tactic. For some of us, it worked. And ironically, those who listened to the son of the morning and rebelled against God *did* become angels to the devil himself.

The second major accusation would have been even more direct and lethal—a bitter indictment against the one individual Lucifer held responsible for standing in his way. "As for the Only Begotten, who has promised to save you—he cannot fulfill his promise. He has committed to become mortal, to live an absolutely sinless life, and then to sacrifice that life willingly. He has promised you what he cannot give. *No one* can do what he has proposed to do. He will fail! And when Jehovah fails, that will be the end, for all of you!"

> For the accuser of our brethren is cast down, which accused them before our God day and night. (Revelation 12:10)

We cannot know for certain what strategy and tactics were employed in that premortal battle. But we do know you and I fought valiantly with the two weapons at our disposal: (1) our absolute faith in the sacred and promised atonement of Jehovah, he who would be Jesus Christ, and (2) our willingness to proclaim it to all who would listen.

> And they overcame him by *the blood of the Lamb*, and *by the word of their testimony*; and they loved not their lives unto the death. (Revelation 12:11; italics added)

*"Unto the death?"* I had always supposed that at least one advantage of fighting a war in heaven is that none of us could be killed in action. But in actuality the death we risked in the premortal world was far more literal than any casualty of war we are familiar with here on earth. For Satan's accusation against the Savior was accurate in one respect. If Jehovah failed, we would never return to our Father in Heaven. We risked spiritual death, more permanent and more devastating than any death imaginable on earth. When we took our stand with our Father and with his Son, we, in effect, deposited all of our hopes and dreams of exaltation in the hands of the Redeemer. In doing so, we literally placed our *eternal lives* on the line.

The war in heaven, whatever form it took, became the qualifier for mortality. It was a test of incredible faith. And you, I, and every person who has ever been born, passed that test and made ourselves worthy. That is how we earned the privilege to be here.

> And they who keep their first estate shall be added upon; and they who keep not their first estate shall not have glory in the same kingdom with those who keep their first estate. (Abraham 3:26)

We, all of us, need to recognize who we are. The youth of Zion, in particular, need to know who they are—and that they kept their first estate. We need to understand that our very presence here in mortality means we once had faith enough to determine the destiny of this world. Because we exercised that faith, and withstood the power of Satan in heaven, we have the capacity to continue to do so on earth. Let us do it.

## The Terms of Defeat

The penalty for Lucifer's sin was nothing less than irreversible exile. The son of the morning and the third part who followed him were denied the privilege of being born into this world and receiving mortal bodies. This crippling sentence meant only one thing.

In the words of Brigham Young,

> Permit me to inquire what was his curse? It was, that he should not increase any more, but come to an end.[1]

Thus, Satan and his hosts were barred forever, not only from the presence of God, but from the privilege of marriage, parenthood, family, and spiritual progression. These stark realities explain the bitterness and rage of Satan toward those of us who have qualified for those blessings.

According to President Boyd K. Packer,

> The adversary is jealous toward all who have the power to beget life. . . . He is impotent. He and those who followed him were cast out and forfeited the right to a mortal body.[2]

Elder Orson Pratt explained the reason for this consequence.

> Could wicked and malicious beings, who have eradicated every feeling of love from their bosoms, be permitted to propagate their species, the offspring would partake of all the evil, wicked, and malicious nature of their parents. . . . It is for this reason that God will not permit the fallen angels to multiply: . . . [and] it is for this reason that none but those who have kept the celestial law will be permitted to multiply after the resurrection.[3]

Satan is determined to destroy our marriages, our families, our future marriages, and our future families. His bitter jealousy rages against all of us who can enjoy those cherished relationships. This insight gives us a glimpse into the adversary's warped vengeance. He seeks to tear down the family because it is central to the Father's plan. But to him it is more and it is personal. He wants you!

Therefore, he entices us to exploit the sacred powers of procreation through sexual transgression. He also invites us to abuse and wear out our bodies through breaking the Word of Wisdom. And at the root of his revenge is the irony that in tempting us to indulge our physical appetites and passions, he allures us to commit sins that are beyond *his* ability to commit. Quite simply, our bodies allow us to sin in ways that he cannot. It is a bitter pill for him to swallow.

The Prophet Joseph Smith said,

> The great principle of happiness consists in having a body. The devil has no body, and herein is his punishment. He is pleased when he can obtain the tabernacle of man, and when cast out by the Savior he asked to go into the herd of swine, showing that he would prefer a swine's body to having none.[4]

Satan's retaliation for this punishment amounts to corporal piracy through the commandeering of bodies that do not belong to him. *Get any body any way you can!* Such highway robbery in the scriptures ranges from the possession or "body snatching" of innocent victims (Mark 9:17–27) to the infestation of a herd of pigs (Mark 5:1–13). Both examples are perfectly in character for Satan and his followers. But more on that later.

## The Unpardonable Sin

Students will sometimes ask if Satan or his followers can ever be forgiven. It is a kind thought—an expression of their charity and goodness. It is commendable that they can hope in their hearts that there might be a measure of mercy extended, even to the devil. So, can devils be forgiven? Our answer, sadly, is no. The scriptures make their fate, and the fate of mortals who sin in the same manner, very clear.

> Thus saith the Lord concerning all those who know my power, and have been made partakers thereof, and suffered themselves through the power of the devil to be overcome, and to deny the truth and defy my power—
>
> They are they who are the sons of perdition, of whom I say that it had been better for them never to have been born;
>
> For they are vessels of wrath, doomed *to suffer the wrath of God, with the devil and his angels in eternity;*

> *Concerning whom I have said there is no forgiveness in this world nor in the world to come.* (D&C 76:31–34; italics added)

The Lord makes the issue pretty cut and dried. He also specifies the crime that would bring such a punishment.

> Having denied the Holy Spirit after having received it, and having denied the Only Begotten Son of the Father, having crucified him unto themselves and put him to an open shame. (D&C 76:35)

Or in other words,

> Who deny the Son after the Father has revealed him. (D&C 74:43)

This rejection of the light, which the scriptures call "open rebellion against God" (Mosiah 2:37), is a willful act, a purposeful denunciation of the Father's will and a deliberate turning to the darkness *after* having been enlightened and illuminated by His glory. The Savior identified this sin as "blasphemy against the Holy Ghost," and made the upcoming final judgment on the matter very clear.

> Wherefore I say unto you, All manner of sin and blasphemy shall be forgiven unto men: but blasphemy against the Holy Ghost shall not be forgiven unto men . . .
> . . . neither in this world, neither in the world to come. (Matthew 12:31–32)

Still, there is often confusion among the Saints on this issue. After all, to varying degrees we have all received the Holy Ghost. And every one of us has acted contrary to that light. We sin. Many have even fallen away. Aren't we all sons of perdition to some extent?

The Prophet Joseph Smith clarifies the nature of the "sin against the Holy Ghost" and explained why so very few qualify for this dishonor.

> What must a man do to commit the unpardonable sin? He must *receive the Holy Ghost, have the heavens opened unto him, and know God, and then sin against Him.* After a man has sinned against the Holy Ghost, there is no repentance for him. *He has got to say that the sun does not shine while he sees it*; he has got to deny Jesus Christ when the heavens have been opened unto him, and to deny the plan of salvation with his eyes open to the truth of it; and from that time he begins to be an enemy.[5]

An explanation for this irrevocable punishment (eternal banishment from the presence of God) is also worth discussing.

It is certainly the nature of our Heavenly Father to forgive. That being true, the reasons that forgiveness cannot be extended to these souls would seem to have more to do with their *inability to repent* than with God's ability or willingness to accept their repentance.

As the author of Hebrews said of the mortal sons of perdition,

> For it is impossible for those who were once enlightened, and have tasted of the heavenly gift, and were made partakers of the Holy Ghost,
>
> And have tasted the good word of God, and the powers of the world to come,
>
> If they shall fall away, *to renew them again unto repentance.* (Hebrews 6:4–6; italics added)

Of these, Joseph Smith said simply,

> You cannot save such persons; you cannot bring them to repentance; they make open war, like the devil, and awful is the consequence.[6]

Such prophetic teachings imply that these transgressors had violated a law of the universe for which no forgiveness or repentance is allowable. It therefore follows that God our Heavenly Father, being subject to those same laws, could not extend forgiveness to them.

But statements of the prophets also suggest that in willfully denying the Holy Ghost and his witness, the rebellious lose the ability to repent and no longer have the capacity for repentance. In other words they *could not* repent and *would not* ask forgiveness—ever.

Speaking of the premortal sons of perdition, President Joseph Fielding Smith said,

> They are banished forever from the presence of God because they have *lost the power of repentance*, for they chose evil by choice after having had the light. While dwelling in the presence of God they knowingly entered into their rebellion.[7]

He also said of their mortal counterparts,

> They have willfully made themselves servants of Satan and servants to him they shall remain forever. *They place themselves beyond the power of repentance and beyond the mercies of God.*[8]

At this point, it should also be made absolutely clear that *only those who sin in this manner are beyond the power of redemption.* It is highly unlikely that anyone reading these words has committed the unpardonable sin and thus qualifies as a son or daughter of perdition. And that means we are all still candidates for the celestial kingdom. The gift of repentance, the grace of God, and the power of the Atonement are available to everyone.

Such is not the case with Satan and his hosts. In their willful and remorseless premortal transgression, Lucifer and the spirits who followed him removed themselves so far from the light that they could not be illuminated again. Lacking the desire or the capacity to partake of the gift of the Atonement, they lost the ability to endure any measure of a kingdom of glory. Without that, only eternal regression awaited them, and nothing but outer darkness could accommodate them. They forfeited their first estate.

> And the great dragon was cast out, that old serpent, called the Devil, and Satan, which deceiveth the whole world: he was cast out into the earth, and his angels were cast out with him. (Revelation 12:9)

## NOTES

1. Brigham Young, in *Journal of Discourses* (London: Latter-day Saints' Book Depot, 1854–86), 1:116.

2. Boyd K. Packer, "Our Moral Environment." *Ensign*, May 1992, 66.

3. Orson Pratt, "Power and Eternity of the Priesthood." *The Seer*, 1853, 156–57.

4. Joseph Fielding Smith, comp., *Teachings of the Prophet Joseph Smith* (Salt Lake City: Deseret Book, 1938), 181.

5. Ibid., 357–58. (Italics added.)

6. Ibid., 358.

7. Joseph Fielding Smith, *Doctrines of Salvation*, comp. Bruce R. McConkie, (Salt Lake City: Bookcraft, 1954–56), 2:219. (Italics added.)

8. Ibid., 2:221. (Italics added.)

# 4

# WARFARE IN THE SECOND ESTATE

Wherefore, he maketh war with the saints of God, and encompasseth them round about. (D&C 76:29)

The end of the War in Heaven was by no means the end of the war. In essence the theater of action had changed, but the war continued. (War always does.) But here on earth, we have been able to better observe, study, and become familiar with Satan through the lens of biblical and world history—history that began when the world was new.

And now the serpent was more subtle than any beast of the field which I, the Lord God, had made.

And Satan put it into the heart of the serpent, . . . and he sought also to beguile Eve, . . . for he knew not the mind of God, wherefore he sought to destroy the world. (Moses 4:5–6)

These verses provide us with a perceptive glimpse into Satan's nature and his modus operandi on earth. Like generals in the "War Room," we need to study his plan of attack, to become acquainted with his strengths and his weaknesses.

**First**, his influence and power are real.
**Second**, his objective is to destroy the world.
**Third**, his approach is subtle.
**Fourth**, his strategy is to beguile—to mislead and deceive by trickery.
**Fifth**, his Achilles' heel, his major weakness, is that he knows not the mind of God.

These five truths give us a keen insight into the operations of Satan and provide us with the intelligence to withstand his maneuvers to mislead us from the truth and take us captive.

# The Plan of Destruction

Having firmly established that Satan is real and that his power is a force to be taken seriously, let us make his aims absolutely clear. He exists to destroy us, our happiness, and everything we live for.

The Prophet Lehi understood the background, nature, and motivation of Satan's warfare in mortality.

> And I, Lehi, according to the things which I have read, must needs suppose that an angel of God, according to that which is written, had fallen from heaven. . . .
>
> And because he had fallen from heaven, and had become miserable forever, he sought also the misery of all mankind. (2 Nephi 2:17–18)

We must never forget that the misery and destruction of man is the predictable motivation behind everything that Satan does.

Niels P. L. Eskildz was converted to the gospel in 1850 in his native Denmark. Although he was severely disabled from a childhood accident, he was determined to answer the call of a prophet and migrate to Zion.

> During the night following his baptism[,] evil spirits seemed to fill the room in which he had retired to sleep. They were not only terribly visible, but he heard voices also, taunting him with having acted foolishly in submitting to baptism and joining the Latter-day Saints. He was told that he had deserted the only friends he ever had, and would find none among the "Mormons," . . . This torment was kept up incessantly until he sought relief in prayer, and three times he got out of bed and tried to pray. . . . Then his fervent pleading unto the Lord for power to withstand the temptation of the evil one, and to hold fast to the truth brought relief to him. The evil spirits gradually, and with apparent reluctance, withdrew, and peace came to his soul, with the assurance that the Lord approved of his embracing the gospel, and that he could safely rely upon the Lord for future guidance.[1]

Many Saints have born witness of the "wrestlings" which preceded or accompanied their decision to be baptized. Though the hosts of Satan may not always be "terribly visible," converts often testify that their confrontations with darkness are as real as they were in the experience of Brother Eskildz.

We have already learned that Satan likes to be present whenever an important spiritual event occurs in our lives. But unlike your favorite grandmother who comes to every special event of your life, Satan's only purpose for attendance is to disrupt. An old proverb says, "Whenever God erects a cathedral, the Devil builds a chapel hard by." (That means right next door.) We find this to be a true principle operating in the scriptures and in our lives. You may be sure that whenever anything really good happens or is about to happen to you, Satan is lurking somewhere in the bushes ready to make his move. It's up to you to prevent him from spoiling things.

Satan's efforts to undermine our personal growth and the progress of God's kingdom on earth are consistent with his sworn objective. From the beginning, his single-minded obsession has been the destruction of the plan, and us along with it. In this passion there is no compromise. There never has been.

President George Q. Cannon described the lengths to which Satan would go to oppose God and frustrate the establishment of his church.

> Satan is determined that God shall not have this earth, and that He shall not reign here; . . . and if he [Satan] could he would shed the blood of every man and woman on the face of the earth, rather than it should go into the hands of God. All those who are connected with him would, if they could, slay every man that stands in their pathway[,] . . . illustrating the truth . . . that "all that will live godly in Christ Jesus, shall suffer persecution"—not *may* suffer it, but they *shall* suffer it.[2]

Satan initiated his violent intentions on earth with an attempt to tear apart the heavenly plan of salvation, which he had failed to derail in the premortal world. In tempting Adam and Eve, his goal was to destroy the family.

Of course, his approach could not be obvious. Such a devious course of destruction had to be undertaken with artful cunning and quiet cleverness. So Satan's subtle assault in the Garden of Eden began with several combined approaches of deliberate fraud—tricks which he continues to use.

Nephi spoke of them:

For behold, at that day shall he *rage* in the hearts of the children of men, and *stir them up to anger* against that which is good.

And others will he *pacify*, and lull them away into carnal security. . . .

And behold, others he *flattereth* away. (2 Nephi 28:20–22; italics added)

Anger, pacifying, flattery. These are the preferred weapons of Satan's arsenal.

## The First Battleground

All of this brings us back to Eden and the target of the adversary's first salvo.

And Satan put it into the heart of the serpent, . . . [following an unsuccessful effort to tempt Adam,] and he sought also to beguile Eve. (Moses 4:6)

"To beguile Eve" to do what? To sin, of course—to break the commandments. And in the simplicity of Eden there were only two—although they were both of critical importance.

The first commandment was revealed to our first parents immediately following their creation.

And I, God, blessed them and said unto them: Be fruitful, and multiply, and replenish the earth. (Moses 2:28)

The powerful plainness of this commandment is unmistakable—*have children and lots of them.* Though modern prophets have emphasized and repeated this principle in our dispensation, there was no need for the Lord to clarify or explain himself to Adam and Eve. Neither of them seemed to have any questions.

The second commandment was equally unequivocal. And yet the Lord pronounced it with an outline of details and a consequence that cause it to stand out in contrast to the first.

And I, the Lord God, commanded [them] saying: Of every tree of the garden thou mayest freely eat,

But of the tree of the knowledge of good and evil, thou shalt not eat of it, *nevertheless, thou mayest choose for thyself, for it is given unto thee; but, remember that I forbid it, for in the day thou eatest thereof thou shalt surely die.* (Moses 3:16–17; italics added)

From these two commandments in mortality's primeval battle-ground, Satan selected the tree of knowledge of good and evil as his initial point of attack.

Satan's favorite weapon of choice, anger, seems to have been worthless to him in the Garden of Eden. The innocent nature of our first parents made rage ineffective. Still, the adversary's approach, like anger, was intended to cloud Eve's perception—to confuse the issue of that "which was good." And he did so in his preliminary approach.

> And he said unto the woman: Yea, hath God said—Ye shall not eat of every tree of the garden? (Moses 4:7)

Listen carefully to the subtle mockery in Satan's question. "You *can* eat everything in the Garden, *can't you*, Eve? Didn't God say that? Hmm?" Eve clarified that there was a small diet restriction in Eden.

> And the woman said unto the serpent: We may eat of the fruit of the trees of the garden;
> But of the fruit of the tree which thou beholdest in the midst of the garden, God hath said—Ye shall not eat of it, neither shall ye touch it, lest ye die. (Moses 4:8–9)

To this objection, Satan smiled and countered with a pacifying half-lie—his second line of strategy.

> Ye shall not surely die. (Moses 4:10)

This was, of course, a comforting deception. After all, it was absolutely true that after partaking of the fruit, Eve would still be among the living. The unstated falsehood in Satan's persuasion was that in the instant that Eve partook she would suffer *spiritual death* for her transgression against the Father's warnings. In addition, the moment she partook of the fruit her body would become mortal. Suddenly subject to death, Eve would, from that instant, begin the long inescapable degeneration that would end in the grave. Like a seasoned used car salesman, Satan failed to mention those little details of the fine print.

Having skirted those obstacles, the adversary then surged ahead with phase three—promises of great reward and no consequence—the same flattery which he employed with success on weaker minds in pre-mortality and has continued to use ever since here on earth.

> For God doth know that in the day ye eat thereof, then your eyes shall be opened, and ye shall be as the gods, knowing good and evil. (Moses 4:11)

Flattery, according to Elder Bruce R. McConkie,

> Is the act of ingratiating oneself into another's confidence by excessive praise, or by insincere speech . . . It includes the raising of false and unfounded hopes; there is always an element of dishonesty attending it.[3]

The combination of *confusing* the issue of good, *pacifying* against the consequences, and the offering of *flattering rewards* certainly seemed to beguile Eve.

> And when the woman saw that the tree was good for food, and that it became pleasant to the eyes, and a tree to be desired to make her wise, she took of the fruit thereof, and did eat. (Moses 4:12)

Eve partook of the fruit for three reasons. Not only was it "good for food" and "pleasant to the eyes," but it included the promise "to make her wise." In fact, the sales pitch, "then your eyes shall be opened" seemed to be the product claim that clinched the deal. Eve was not acting out of curiosity or a want of mere satisfaction. Satan appealed to an innate longing within Eve to progress, to be "as the gods, knowing good from evil." She desired wisdom. Interestingly, her response to Satan's enticements was surprisingly wise.

## Satan's Weakness and Initial Defeat on Earth

For thousands of years, a world in apostasy has viewed that initial confrontation as a victory for the dark side—Satan: 1, God: zip. But this point tally merely reflects a historical lack of understanding of the Father's plan. Like Laman and Lemuel, the scorekeepers of the world "knew not the dealings of that God who had created them" (1 Nephi 2:12).

Satan's deception was both clever and understated—two strengths at which he excels. However, we know that Eve wasn't as fooled as we've been taught by apostate Christianity. Remember, there were *two* commandments in Eden. And as Lehi taught, our first parents had to transgress one to keep the other. The conflict between the two created a choice—setting agency in motion. They needed to partake of the fruit and become mortal in order to "multiply and replenish the earth."

And now, behold, if Adam [and Eve] had not transgressed [they] would not have fallen. . . .

And they would have had no children. (2 Nephi 2:22–23)

History's initial experiment in agency—the decision between two commandments—was not an easy exercise for Adam and Eve. Yet their best choice of obedience and their sincere desire to do right were Satan's ultimate undoing.

The record makes it clear that Satan was bound to lose, and even tells us why.

He sought also to beguile Eve, for *he knew not* the mind of God. (Moses 4:6; italics added)

In the end, the tables were turned and it was Satan, not Eve, who was fooled. This was according to the blueprint of the Father. Adam and Eve partook of the fruit, became mortal, and began their journey of progression, as well as ours.

Adam fell that men might be; and men are, that they might have joy. (2 Nephi 2:25)

Instead of destroying the plan, Satan not only furthered it, but began to play an integral part in it.

For it must needs be, that there is an opposition in all things. (2 Nephi 2:11)

Rather than becoming Satan's first victim, Mother Eve became his first mortal nemesis. She performed magnificently! And in possession of the knowledge between good and evil, her advice to Adam was to follow her example.

[She] also gave unto her husband with her, and he did eat. (Moses 4:12)

Adam and Eve were both awesome—the first heroes in world history. But "the mother of all living" (Moses 4:26) was the driving force in the victory of Eden. In retaliation, the adversary has never forgiven it, nor forgotten it. Hugh Nibley explains,

Ever since then, Satan has "had it in for women." She [Eve] thwarted his plan of destruction and she recognized him. . . . This grudge, which at times rages as a pitched battle, continues today.[4]

Women and young women need to be intensely aware of this pitched battle. There indeed is a "war on women" and it is being waged by Satan. It is being staged in the media and in music, within magazines on the newsstands, and on every front of today's pop culture. The strategy and tactics are clever and the objective is clear—to blur the nature and identity of God's precious daughters and to obscure their sense of divine destiny.

However, God was well acquainted with Satan's vindictive nature. From the Garden of Eden, our Father laid permanent boundaries against him in a decree designed to protect us as well as Eve.

> And I will put enmity between thee and the woman, between thy seed and her seed; and he shall bruise thy head, and thou shalt bruise his heel. (Moses 4:21)

That enmity—the instinctive revulsion we (and especially women) feel for Satan—seems to be one of the multitude of gifts we receive from the Atonement, "the bruising of Satan's head." Today as in the past, the simple power of testimony and the blood of the Lamb serve as the weapons that determine our victory.

# NOTES

1. George C. Lambert, *Treasures in Heaven* (Salt Lake City: Juvenile Instructors Office, 1914), 22–23.

2. George Q. Cannon, *Journal of Discourses* (London: Latter-day Saints' Book Depot, 1854–86), 24:375–76.

3. Bruce R. McConkie, *Mormon Doctrine*, 2nd ed. (Salt Lake City: Bookcraft, 1966), 287.

4. Hugh Nibley, in Beverly Campbell, "Mother Eve, Mentor for Today's Woman: A Heritage of Honor," *Collegium Aesculpium* 12, no. 1 (1994): 43.

# 5

# A Revised Strategy on Earth

Thus began mortality—a period of growth and testing for the children of God. To make that growth possible, and to make that testing endurable, Father in Heaven declared his intention to provide a Savior for us. The mighty efforts of this Savior, this Mediator, this Redeemer promised to reconcile us to God, and correct the effects of the Fall. The Atonement of Jesus Christ became the critical key, and in fact, the hope of our salvation and exaltation.

Our first parents taught their children of the promised sacrifice from the Only Begotten, and all that it meant to them. However, not all of Adam and Eve's seed have taken advantage of that blessing.

> Satan came among them, saying: I am also a son of God; and he commanded them saying: Believe it not; and they believed it not and they loved Satan more than God. And men began from that time forth to be carnal, sensual, and devilish. (Moses 5:13)

The damning choice of some of their first children was a severe disappointment to Adam and Eve, who had anticipated better things for their family. (Our parents always do.) Faithfully our first parents "ceased not to call upon God." (Moses 5:16). They were blessed with another son, for whom they had great expectations.

> She [Eve] conceived and bare Cain, and said: I have gotten a man from the Lord; wherefore he may not reject his words. (Moses 5:16)

Cain! What an incredible disappointment! It's hard to believe that any of us could bring the grief to our parents that Cain brought to

Adam and Eve. Like his older brothers and sisters, Cain also deliber-
ately rejected God.

> But behold, Cain hearkened not, saying: Who is the Lord that I should
> know him?
> . . . And Cain loved Satan more than God. (Moses 5:16, 18)

The principle we learn from the example of our early cousins is a
powerful one that the scriptures and the prophets emphasize. Youth
and adults alike need to understand the *destructiveness of rebellion* and
the edifying *power of obedience*. We become vulnerable to the powers
of darkness when we allow our pride and stubbornness to turn us from
God. That is the lesson we should have learned from the Grand Council—a lesson we will learn again from Cain.

> And he [Lucifer] became Satan, yea, even the devil, the father of all lies,
> to deceive and to blind men, and to lead them captive at his will, *even
> as many as would not hearken unto my voice.* (Moses 4:4; italics added)

The Prophet Joseph Smith made this point clear:

> The devil has no power over us only as we permit him. The moment
> we revolt at anything which comes from God, the devil takes power.[1]

Historically, the "buffetings of Satan" (D&C 104:9–10) are consistent as a consequence of rebellion.

Sidney Rigdon was left to preside over the Church at Kirtland in
1831 while Joseph resided for a time at Hiram, Ohio. On one occasion
Sidney preached that because of the faithlessness of the Saints the keys
of the kingdom had been taken from them. This caused great confusion and anxiety in the community.

> The word went abroad among the people immediately that Sidney was
> going to expose "Mormonism."
> Joseph came up to Kirtland a few days afterwards and held a
> meeting in a large barn. . . .
> Joseph arose in our midst and spoke in mighty power saying: I can
> contend with wicked men and devils. . . . No power can pluck those
> keys from me, except the power that gave them to me; . . . But for what
> Sidney has done, the devil shall handle him as one man handles another.
> [Upon hearing of Joseph's words, Sidney] replied: "Is it possible
> that I have been so deceived?"

About three weeks after this, Sidney was lying on his bed alone. An unseen power lifted him from his bed, threw him across the room, and tossed him from one side of the room to the other . . . from the effects of which Sidney was laid up for five or six weeks. Thus was Joseph's prediction in regard to him verified.[2]

The New Testament, and the annals of the restored Church,' cite many instances of physical possession—often as a result of sin and disobedience. (Disease and infirmity associated with evil spirits have also sometimes been attributed to transgression.)[3] Stories of demonic hostile takeovers, in both scripture and historical lore, have become the staple of our cultural familiarity with Satan. They are dramatic and illustrate the power of the adversary, and the determination of his followers to claim bodies that are not their own.

As they went out, behold, they brought to him [Jesus] a dumb man possessed with a devil.

And when the devil was cast out, the dumb spake: and the multitudes marveled, saying, It was never so seen in Israel. (Matthew 9:32–33)

But sensational experiences such as these miss the point. According to the warnings of modern prophets, we need to be most wary of the adversary's ability to "possess" our lives (exemplified in the life of Cain). Satan desires to have us (Moses 5:23). Through our rebellion, he can take control of us as completely as he took control of Cain.

In response to so-called spiritual phenomena in the early days of the Church, the Lord revealed through the Prophet Joseph Smith,

Hearken, O ye elders of my church, and give ear to the voice of the living God; and attend to the words of wisdom which shall be given unto you . . . as touching the church, and the spirits which have gone abroad in the earth.

Behold, verily I say unto you, that there are many spirits which are false spirits, which have gone forth in the earth.

And also Satan hath sought to deceive you, that he might overthrow you. (D&C 50:1–3)

It is instructive to identify many of the "spirits which have gone abroad in the earth" with the characteristics of darkness that often afflict and torment our souls. The scriptures speak variously of the spirit of bondage, the spirit of persecution, the spirit of anger, the spirit of jealousy, the spirit of fear, or the spirit of contention. We often refer to the spirit of rebellion, depression, disobedience, envy, selfishness, malice, cruelty, or hatred. There are indeed many false spirits that have "gone abroad in the earth." Satan is the source of all of them. And we often allow ourselves to be possessed by them. Yet the Savior can cast them from us if we will turn our hearts over to him.

President John Taylor, speaking of the rebellious, said,

> When they [the Saints] begin to murmur and complain, to find fault and to give way to improper influences, they give place to the devil, *and he takes possession just as fast and as far as he can*, and forces upon them feelings, ideas and principles that are at variance with the law and order, and the word and will of God.[4]

It always comes down to the issue of agency and personal choice. Whenever we hearken to the Holy Ghost, we will be blessed, delivered from evil, and filled with the Spirit. However, if we allow Satan to have power over our minds and hearts, if we permit him to lead us astray, we will be filled with an entirely different kind of spirit, which will have dominion over us.

## The Universal Key to Deliverance

The ideal way to escape the adversary and his possessive spirits has been stressed by every prophet who has ever lived. President George Q. Cannon taught this familiar mandate.

> In view of this, what should be our course? Perfect, implicit, unquestioned obedience to our Father and God. . . . We should not by thought, by word, by action, by any example, by any influence, lend any assistance to this being that is opposed to our God, and who is our deadly enemy, and the deadly enemy of every son and daughter of God.[5]

Pay attention to that imperative: "Perfect, implicit, unquestioned obedience to our Father and God."

President George Albert Smith expressed this same principle in the simplest of terms.

> There is a line of demarcation well defined between the Lord's territory and the devil's territory. If you will stay on the Lord's side of the line

you will be under his influence and will have no desire to do wrong; but if you cross to the devil's side of that line one inch you are in the tempter's power and if he is successful, you will not be able to think or even reason properly because you will have lost the Spirit of the Lord.[6]

He then reiterated,

There is safety for us only on the Lord's side of the line.[7]

The Savior understood clearly which side he was on and provided us with the ideal example in resisting temptation. It was, in essence, a rematch of the battles from the War in Heaven—one on one.

And when the tempter came to him, he said, *If thou be the Son of God*, command these stones be made bread.

But he [Jesus] answered and said, *It is written*, Man shall not live by bread alone, but by every word that proceedeth out of the mouth of God. (Matthew 4:3–4; italics added)

Round one—Jesus.

Then the devil taketh him up into the holy city, and setteth him on a pinnacle of the temple,

And saith unto him, *If thou be the Son of God*, cast thyself down: for it is written, He shall give his angels charge concerning thee: and in their hands they shall bear thee up . . .

Jesus said unto him, *It is written again*, Thou shalt not tempt the Lord thy God. (Matthew 4:5–7; italics added)

Round two—Jesus.

Again, the devil taketh him up into an exceeding high mountain, and sheweth him all the kingdoms of the world, and the glory of them;

And saith unto him, All these things will I give thee, if thou wilt fall down and worship me.

Then saith Jesus unto him, Get thee hence, Satan: for *it is written*, Thou shalt worship the Lord thy God, and him only shalt thou serve. (Matthew 4:8–10; italics added)

Round three (predictably)—Jesus.

Notice the following in each of these contests:
(1) Satan challenges the Savior to prove his identity. "If thou be the

Son of God" is his favorite taunt. This is playground mentality. "Oh, yeah? Prove it!" But no one ever suggested that Satan was mature.

(2) Each time the Savior answers the challenge from the scriptures. Jesus's repeated declaration of "It is written" bears witness to us that the word of God will bring us wisdom and power. That power is literal.

(3) Finally, Jesus Christ always defeats Satan's efforts. He is consistently the victor in every match and rematch—no exceptions. The Savior always emerges as "the winner and still champion." The question is, will we?

> Then the devil leaveth him, and, behold, angels came and ministered unto him. (Matthew 4:11)

Jesus Christ provides us with the formula for success. In the words of the Apostle James,

> Submit yourselves therefore to God. Resist the devil, and he will flee from you. (James 4:7)

The Prophet Joseph Smith also reaffirmed the power of righteous living as the means to overcoming Satan.

> As well might the devil seek to dethrone Jehovah, as overthrow an innocent soul that resists everything which is evil.[8]

"Resisting the devil" and the principle of obedience, "perfect, implicit, unquestioned obedience," function as twin swords in our hands: the keys to victory over the powers of Satan.

## Recruited into the Ranks of the Adversary

Cain rejected these key principles. Rebelling against God, he clung to the adversary, making himself a prime target for Satan's favorite deceptions. He became the devil's perfect disciple and perfect dupe.

> And Cain loved Satan more than God. And Satan commanded him, saying: Make an offering unto the Lord.
> And in process of time it came to pass that Cain brought of the fruit of the ground an offering unto the Lord.
> And Abel, he also brought of the firstlings of his flock, and of the fat thereof. And the Lord had respect unto Abel, and to his offering;
> But unto Cain, and to his offering, he had not respect. (Moses 5:18–21)

This is how Satan sets us up as suckers. He revels in comparison and jealousy—and then stacks the deck. He commanded Cain to make a sacrifice unto the Lord that he knew would be rejected, and of course it was.

> Now Satan knew this, and it pleased him. And Cain was very wroth, and his countenance fell. (Moses 5:21) (Did you recognize the employment of anger?)

It was then that God got involved. He certainly didn't have to and wasn't invited to do so. Unencumbered by any pride in the matter, Heavenly Father lovingly encouraged Cain to return to him. It is an incredibly selfless gesture on the part of the God of the Universe. We would all be wise to hear and heed his compassionate warnings.

> If thou doest well, thou shalt be accepted. And if thou doest not well, sin lieth at the door, and Satan *desireth to have thee*; and *except thou shalt hearken unto my commandments*, I will deliver thee up, and it shall be unto thee *according to his desire*. (Moses 5:23; italics added)

God and Satan operate very differently. While Satan is consistently spiteful and manipulative, our Heavenly Father is eternally loving, encouraging, and forgiving.

Again, obedience is the simple key to deliverance—and disobedience is the portent of our doom. In defiance against God we surrender ourselves to the complete manipulation of the adversary. "Satan desireth to have thee . . . and it shall be according to his desire" (Moses 5:23). Once Cain had rebelled, he became an easy mark for Satan's incitement to rage, his pacifying strategy, and his flattering words.

President John Taylor re-created their interview this way:

> Then Satan came again and whispered to Cain, I could have told you all about it before; God is an unrighteous God; he gathers where he has not strewn, he reaps where he has not sown. He was unjust to me in heaven, and therefore I rebelled against him; and I advise you to do so also. And Cain listened to the advice of Satan, and as the devil was a murderer and a liar from the beginning, so he induced Cain to become the same.[9]

Satanic sympathy serves as a soothing balm to our wounded pride. The adversary works this consolation like a craftsman to seduce us to his will. Oozing with flattery and falsehood, Satan played Cain like a harp.

> And Satan said unto Cain: Swear unto me by thy throat, and if thou tell it thou shalt die; and swear thy brethren by their heads, and by the living God, that they tell it not; . . . and this day I will deliver thy brother Abel into thine hands.
>
> And Satan sware unto Cain that he would do according to his commands. And all these things were done in secret. (Moses 5:29–30)

Thus, enticing Cain with demonic oaths and worldly promises, the adversary led him from one abomination to another until he committed the most tragic and irreversible of sins—total rejection of God through denial of the Holy Ghost, and murder.

> And Cain gloried in that which he had done, saying: I am free. (Moses 5:33)

No statement could have been more self-deceptive, or more patently false. In a short time the judgment of God sentenced Cain to be "a fugitive and a vagabond in the earth" (Genesis 4:14), driven out from the face of the Lord and shut out from his presence. Thus was Satan's fraud complete.

As Satan maneuvered with Cain "to have him . . . according to his desire," likewise does he subtly work to enslave God's children in all ages.

> And he leadeth them by the neck with a flaxen cord, until he bindeth them with his strong cords forever. (2 Nephi 26:22)
>
> And thus the devil cheateth their souls, and leadeth them away carefully down to hell. (2 Nephi 28:21)
>
> And thus he whispereth in their ears, until he grasps them with his awful chains, from whence there is no deliverance. (2 Nephi 28:22)

Satan begins with the most enticing of sins and the most soothing of rewards ("a flaxen cord") while binding us subtly with entertainments and appetites ("strong cords"). Social smoking and drinking, recreational drug use, and casual pornography will invariably turn into alcoholism, addictions, and sexual obsessions that will destroy our lives and the lives of those around us. All the while Satan continues to gently beguile us ("he whispereth in [our] ears"), making the journey to damnation very pleasant ("and leadeth . . . away carefully down to hell") until we realize we are trapped ("he grasps . . . with his awful chains").

If we read of such a physical abduction in the papers or saw it on the news, we would be horrified and nauseated by the violence of the crime. Yet this brutal kidnapping of the soul is just as cruel and sadistic. Satan's crimes are beyond imagination because they are an assault on that part of us which is eternal—an assault "from whence there is no deliverance."

Elder Sterling W. Sill of the Seventy shared a classic story of fiction to illustrate Satan's standard procedure of gradual damnation.

> We remember the old legend of Faust, who made a deal that if Satan would serve him for twenty-four years, punishing Faust's enemies, aiding his friends, and helping him to have a good time, then Faust would forever deliver up his soul to Satan. To Faust this may have seemed like a great idea. Twenty-four years was a long time, and whatever happened beyond that time seemed to be very unimportant.
>
> Accordingly, the twenty-four years began and Faust had many wonderful experiences. But almost before he was aware of it he was told, "Thine hour is come." This was the first time that Faust had ever thought about the reckoning. Then he said to himself, "Ah Faustus, thou hast now but one bare hour to live and then thou must be damned eternally."
>
> For the first time Faust knew that he had cheated himself and he wanted to change the situation, but it was too late. Then he prayed and said, "Oh, God, if thou canst have no mercy on my soul, at least grant some end to my incessant pain. Let Faustus live in hell a thousand years, or even a hundred thousand, but at last be saved." He knew, however, that according to his bargain, even this could never be. He sat and watched the clock tick off the seconds and finally, just before the hour struck, the last words of Faust before he died were: "Faustus is gone to hell."
>
> Faust had been robbed of his eternal life by a deception in his own perspective. And this problem is one that we should all be concerned about.[10]

Indeed we should all be concerned—and vigilant. Satan and his hosts are zealously dedicated to our destruction. In this effort they will never rest, they will never sleep, and they will never stop. It is a war in which we will be engaged "until the Great Jehovah shall say the work is done."[11]

# NOTES

1. Joseph Fielding Smith, comp., *Teachings of the Prophet Joseph Smith* (Salt Lake City: Deseret Book, 1938), 181.

2. Hyrum L. Andrus and Helen Mae Andrus, *They Knew the Prophet* (Salt Lake City: Bookcraft, 1974), 67.

3. The argument that infirmity or possession can be a consequence of sin is justified by many statements of the modern prophets cited in this chapter. John 5:14 provides us with Jesus's counsel to the infirm man, healed at the pool of Bethesda. "Afterward Jesus findeth him in the temple, and said unto him, Behold, thou art made whole: sin no more, lest a worse thing come upon thee." (See also Matthew 9:2 and John 9:2.)

4. John Taylor, in *Journal of Discourses* (London: Latter-day Saints' Book Depot, 1854–86), 26:131. (Italics added.)

5. George Q. Cannon, in *Journal of Discourses*, 25:302.

6. *Teachings of the Presidents of the Church—George Albert Smith* (Salt Lake City: Church of Jesus Christ of Latter-day Saints, 2011), 191.

7. Ibid.

8. Joseph Fielding Smith, *Teachings of the Prophet Joseph Smith*, 226.

9. John Taylor, in *Journal of Discourses*, 22:301.

10. Sterling W. Sill, *Thy Kingdom Come* (Salt Lake City: Deseret Book, 1975), 75.

11. Joseph Smith, *History of the Church of Jesus Christ of Latter-day Saints*, 6 vols., ed. B. H. Roberts, 2nd ed. rev. (Salt Lake City: Deseret Book, 1957), 4:540.

# 6

# THE POWERS OF DARKNESS

Satan's strength is in the subtle approach. But to assume that the magnitude of his power is represented by an inconspicuous style is to underestimate him. True, he prefers understated deception. Still, occasionally he cannot resist theatrics in his efforts to have us. Unlike the Holy Ghost, he does not limit himself to the still, small voice.

Moses discovered this characteristic of the adversary in an experience that closely followed the revelation at the burning bush. The Pearl of Great Price tells that

> Moses was caught up into an exceedingly high mountain,
>     And he saw God face to face, and he talked with him, and the glory of God was upon Moses; therefore Moses could endure his presence. (Moses 1:1–2)

The scripture makes it clear that Moses could not have endured the Almighty's presence had not the glory of God prepared him for the experience.

> For I should have withered and died in his presence; but his glory was upon me; and I beheld his face, for I was transfigured before him. (Moses 1:11)

This is all very important information considering what happens next.

> And it came to pass that . . . Satan came tempting him, saying: Moses, son of man, worship me. (Moses 1:12)

We've seen this before. It is all an unsurprising, standard procedure from the adversary. Moses's response, however, is anything but predictable:

> And it came to pass that Moses looked upon Satan and said: Who art thou? For behold, I am a son of God, in the similitude of his Only Begotten; and where is thy glory, that I should worship thee? (Moses 1:13)

Wow! Are you kidding me? This was an unbelievable confrontation. The adversary could not have been more insulted and enraged. By any stretch of the imagination, this was a painful "in your face" face-off for Satan—one in which Moses becomes one of the great heroes of scripture.

First, in no uncertain terms, he clarifies his own relationship with God. ("I am a son of God.") Second, he questions Satan's authority to confuse that relationship. ("Who art thou?") Ouch! And finally, Moses pours a generous dose of salt into some old, festering wounds through his reverence for the Only Begotten and his flat refusal to worship Satan—Lucifer's fondest unfulfilled ambition. ("Where is thy glory, that I should worship thee?")

Moses continues to challenge Satan—instructing him on his spiritual inadequacies and reminding him of what has always been the first commandment:

> For behold, I could not look upon God, except his glory should come upon me. . . . But I can look upon thee in the natural man. Is it not so, surely?
>
> . . . Where is thy glory, for it is darkness unto me? And I can judge between thee and God; for God said unto me: Worship God, for him only shalt thou serve. (Moses 1:14–15)

*That* had to hurt. It upsets Satan to be found out, and he's always been quite sensitive about our unwillingness to adore him. But Moses is not through. Or better said, he *is* through. As far as he is concerned, the interview is over as he commands the adversary twice to leave.

> Get thee hence, Satan; deceive me not; for God said unto me: Thou art after the similitude of mine Only Begotten.
>
> And he also gave me commandments . . . saying: Call upon God in the name of mine Only Begotten, and worship me.

> And again Moses said: I will not cease to call upon God . . . for his glory has been upon me, wherefore I can judge between him and thee. Depart hence, Satan. (Moses 1:16–18)

As was the case with Moses, our righteousness and the light it brings into our lives allows us to discern the darkness of the adversary and identify him by that light. Satan does not enjoy the glare of that illumination. As Moses reiterates both his commitment to God and his reverence for the Only Begotten, he obviously hits some tender nerves. Satan's reaction is explosive and violent:

> And now, when Moses had said these words, Satan cried with a loud voice, and ranted upon the earth, and commanded, saying: I am the Only Begotten, worship me. (Moses 1:19)

So much for subtlety. Moses responded with appropriate terror, and an outpouring of faith:

> And it came to pass that Moses began to fear exceedingly; and as he began to fear, he saw the bitterness of hell. Nevertheless, calling upon God, he received strength, and he commanded, saying: Depart from me, Satan, for this one God only will I worship, which is the God of glory. (Moses 1:20)

Notice too that for the third time, Moses rebukes the adversary, this time with the most solemn pronouncement, but without effect. Finally we read,

> And now Satan began to tremble, and the earth shook; and Moses received strength, and called upon God, saying: In the name of the Only Begotten, depart hence, Satan. (Moses 1:21)

Casting aside any pretensions of restraint, Satan here demonstrates a very real and potent power to shake the earth and strike well-justified fear into the heart of Moses. And observe too that it was a literal power, a power that could only be dispelled by a higher authority—the power of Jesus Christ and his Atonement.

> And it came to pass that Satan cried with a loud voice, with weeping, and wailing, and gnashing of teeth; and he departed hence. (Moses 1:22)

Just as Moses was commanded to "call upon God in the name

of [the] Only Begotten" (Moses 1:17), so God has instructed us to call on the name of Jesus Christ for deliverance in our confrontations with Satan. And Jesus Christ always wins. Like Moses, we may come to recognize and contrast the light and the darkness through experience, careful attention to the whisperings of the Spirit, and reliance on the Savior.

My wife, Diane, understands satanic adversity as well as the power of faith gathered from such experiences. When I asked Diane to marry me after a few short months of dating, she said yes. Her answer was based on a powerful spiritual witness, completely unrelated to the lure of my rugged good looks and my sculpted, muscular physique. However, immediately upon accepting my proposal, her mind and her heart became shrouded with doubts—serious, violent, debilitating doubts about time and eternity with me. (Yeah, go figure!) A dark shadow enveloped her life for weeks.

It wasn't until she received a priesthood blessing from a caring bishop that the shadow lifted and she recognized the source of her confusion. She realized she had already obtained her answer, and that her depressed feelings were more than "second thoughts." Her passage through darkness had been the result of Satan making an all-out assault to destroy her—and us. With that comprehension, and the acknowledgment of her previous spiritual confirmation, she went forward with faith and never looked back. *I* was the nervous one on our wedding day.

Years later the experience repeated itself. Diane and I had made a decision to adopt two Russian teenagers. As a seminary teacher I certainly should have known better. But, contrary to traditional wisdom, the Spirit confirmed powerfully to our hearts that we were indeed to invite two young people from Siberia into our family.

As soon as we committed ourselves to the long process of adoption, a spirit of gloom and depression filled our home—a spirit which might have been easily misinterpreted as the "stupor of thought" spoken of in the scriptures. However, after languishing under the burden of its negative weight for a short time, Diane recognized the influence of Satan. She had been here before, and the Holy Ghost brought it to her remembrance. Satan was revealed. She was no longer confused. From there she took charge. Standing alone in our kitchen that morning, she cleared her throat and challenged the evil spirit aloud.

"Okay. I know who you are and I know what you're trying to do. So you might as well quit because nothing you do is going to make any difference. We're going to go through with this adoption."

She said the relief was almost instantaneous. The darkness and confusion dispersed, replaced by the calm, peace, and power of the Spirit. Satan and his followers shrink from the glorious light of faith and truth. "Resist the devil, and he will flee from you" (James 4:7).

# The Priesthoods of Good and Evil

We know that Satan is capable of demonstrating an awesome show of real power and influence—beyond his standard ability to frustrate, discourage, and cause anxiety. The Apostle Paul described him appropriately as "the prince of the power of the air" (Ephesians 2:2).

Elder Joseph Fielding Smith said as much.

> Satan has great knowledge and thereby can exercise authority and to some extent control the elements, when some greater power does not intervene.[1]

If permitted by our Heavenly Father, the adversary has the ability to employ the forces of nature to the injury of men. The story of Job and his physical suffering demonstrates that Satan has the power to make our lives very unpleasant.

Presented as a poetic parable, the Book of Job begins with a dinner reception, so to speak, hosted by our Heavenly Father.

> Now there was a day when the sons of God came to present themselves before the Lord, and Satan came also among them.
>
> And the Lord said unto Satan, Hast thou considered my servant Job, that there is none like him in the earth, a perfect and upright man, one that feareth God, and escheweth evil? (Job 1:6,8)

God goes on and on, with all kinds of good things to say about Job. And why not? Job is "perfect and upright." "There is none like him." (Wouldn't it be nice if God could so brag about us.) Satan, however, is not impressed.

> Then Satan answered the Lord, and said, Doth Job fear God for nought?
>
> Hast not thou made an hedge about him, and about his house, and about all that he hath on every side? Thou hast blessed the work of his hands, and his substance is increased in the land. (Job 1:9–10)

"Why in the world shouldn't Job be righteous?" counters Satan. "He has everything he wants and needs. He is the richest man in the east. And as a reward for his goodness you continue to bless him." Now comes the challenge:

> But put forth thine hand now, and touch all that he hath, and he will curse thee to thy face. (Job 1:11)

This is an "I double-dog dare ya" proposition—again, straight from the playground. "Let's see how good Job is if you take away all his blessings."

> And the Lord said unto Satan, Behold, all that he hath is in thy power; only upon himself put not forth thine hand. (Job 1:12)

"All right," agrees the Lord. "It's a deal. Go ahead and take away all of Job's physical possessions. Anything goes. (You just aren't allowed to hurt Job.) You'll see how good he is."

"Done," says Satan, smiling.

> So Satan went forth from the presence of the Lord. (Job 1:12)

In the next few verses of chapter one, Job loses everything—seven thousand sheep, three thousand camels, five hundred yoke of oxen, and five hundred she asses—virtually everything he has—along with practically all of the servants who cared for them. Not content with that handiwork, Satan also kills Job's seven sons and three daughters in an "accident." (Satan loves accidents.) All things considered it's been a bad day at the office for Job. Yet his response is a classic statement of incredible faith in God.

> Naked came I out of my mother's womb, and naked shall I return thither; the Lord gave, and the Lord hath taken away; blessed be the name of the Lord. (Job 1:21)

Wow! Job passed the test with flying colors. His valiance and faith represent a pretty humiliating defeat for Satan—an issue that God reminds him of at the next family reunion:

> Again there was a day when the sons of God came to present themselves before the Lord, and Satan came also among them to present himself before the Lord. . . .
> And the Lord said unto Satan, Hast thou considered my servant

Job, that there is none like him in the earth, a perfect and upright man, one that feareth God, and escheweth evil? And still he holdeth fast his integrity, although thou movedst me against him, to destroy him without cause. (Job 2:1, 3)

God is absolutely delighted here. Figuratively speaking, he's spiking the ball in the end zone. "What do you think of Job now?" he rejoices. "Didn't I tell you he's awesome?" Still, Satan is unimpressed.

And Satan answered the Lord, and said, Skin for skin, yea, all that a man hath will he give for his life.

But put forth thine hand now, and touch his bone and his flesh, and he will curse thee to thy face. (Job 2:4–5)

A bad sport on the playground of eternity, Satan refuses to admit that he lost the challenge. Instead, he issues another dare, which the Lord confidently accepts.

And the Lord said unto Satan, Behold, he is in thine hand; but save his life.

So went Satan forth from the presence of the Lord. (Job 2:6–7)

Over the remaining forty chapters of the book, the adversary proceeds to do his worst, afflicting Job with festering boils, worms, nightmares, unanswered prayers, disloyal friends, accusations of iniquity, and alienation from society. Satan's only restriction (probably a very disappointing one) is that he is forbidden to take Job's life. And yet through it all Job expresses a consistent faithfulness, reflected in his initial praise and submission to God.

What? Shall we receive good at the hand of God, and shall we not receive evil? In all this did not Job sin with his lips. (Job 2:10)

Indeed, God's appraisal of Job is accurate; "There is none like him in the earth" (Job 2:3).

Now, the purpose of this story is not to suggest for an instant that our Heavenly Father holds regular garden parties for his children or makes personal wagers with Lucifer. The Book of Job is a poetic/dramatic presentation of the life of a real person who struggled with adversity and emerged victorious, teaching us timeless principles.

In the end, Job is rewarded double-fold for his faithfulness and we are taught *the eternal value of suffering*. But for our purposes, the book also teaches us the simple reality that Satan has power, that he is allowed to wield it only by the permission of God, and that his power has specific limitations.

Verifying the account in Job, Brigham Young suggests a universal demonic source for all physical miseries:

> You never felt a pain and ache, or felt disagreeable, or uncomfortable in your bodies and minds, but what an evil spirit was present causing it. Do you realize that . . . any pain in the system, from the crown of the head to the soles of the feet, is put there by the devil?[2]

Giving the adversary credit for every physical ailment that afflicts us—from indigestion to a migraine headache—may seem extreme. But we have to remind ourselves that Satan *is* the "god" of this fallen world. Elder James E. Talmage provides us with a similar (though tempered) declaration:

> He seeks to molest and hinder mankind in good efforts, by tempting to sin; *or it may be by imposing sickness, or possibly death.*[3]

In any event, Elder Talmage (and all the prophets) make it clear that our Heavenly Father sets the limits on Satan's ability to do us harm:

> Yet in all these malignant doings, he can go no farther than the transgressions of the victim may enable him, or the wisdom of God may permit; and at any time he may be checked by the superior power.[4]

Satan's restricted power to cause suffering and death was also authenticated in this account by President Heber J. Grant:

> When my wife died, I took my oldest three daughters to Boston, New York and other places in the hope that the sorrow caused by the death of their mother might be forgotten. When we reached Washington, two of them were taken ill with diphtheria. They were as sick as any children I have ever seen. The younger of the two was so low [ill] . . . I felt sure she was going to die. . . . I prayed for her life, and shed bitter tears of humiliation. While praying, the inspiration came to me that if I would send for the elders who were in Washington and have them administer to her, she would live. . . . I know that I was shedding tears of sorrow, fear and anguish while I was praying, and I know that immediately thereafter I received the witness of the Spirit that my little girl should live, and I shed tears of unbounded joy and gratitude. . . .

When George Q. Cannon laid his hands upon my daughter's head to seal the anointing . . . he made a statement that I have never heard before or since, in all my life, in any prayer. He said in substance: "The adversary, the destroyer, has decreed your death and made public announcement that you shall die, but by the authority of the priesthood of the Living God, we rebuke the decree of the adversary, and say that you shall live, and not die."[5]

The healing invoked by that blessing was immediate and powerful. The little girl steadily improved and the crisis was past. However, over the days and weeks of her convalescence, Elder Grant wondered about the wording of the priesthood prayer—that the adversary had announced the girl's death. The statement was not made clear until the family was about to return home.

As we were leaving the boardinghouse, the gentleman whose wife had been in charge there . . . said to me: "Mr. Grant, I have a joke on my wife. She believes in spiritualism, and when your little girls were taken sick she went to her medium." The medium . . . told her the following story:

That she saw two little girls in her house; she saw the older one taken sick, . . . then the other little girl became sick, nigh unto death; she finally saw the first little girl recover and the second little girl die. . . .

But through the priesthood of the Living God, the decree of the adversary was rebuked, and my daughter lived.[6]

So the power of Satan, significant though it may be, is definitely restricted.

Joseph Smith said,

Wicked spirits have their bounds, limits, and laws by which they are governed.[7]

Perhaps Brigham Young expressed the entire issue best:

The power of the devil is limited; the power of God is unlimited.[8]

Foremost of the realities of the universe is that God, our Heavenly Father, is, and always will be, in control. It is a power he never relinquishes.

The period of the Great Apostasy offers us an example. Satan scored what he may have felt was the ultimate victory in the crucifixion of the Savior—"thou shalt bruise his heel" (Moses 4:21). But as in all of his efforts, he only furthered the Atonement, the plan of salvation, and his own ultimate destruction—"and he shall bruise thy head" (Moses 4:21). Satan "knew not the mind of God" (Moses 4:6). Still, the powers of darkness did *seem* to be temporarily victorious at Golgotha.

Yet throughout the dark ages that followed, Satan's influence, though considerable, was not unlimited. For hundreds of years his power had a specific ceiling.

Elder Orson Pratt teaches,

> The Lord will not suffer him [Satan] to go any further than he permits; and when the people have not the *Gospel* and *Priesthood* in their midst, and light and knowledge from the heavens, He will not suffer the devil to show forth his power to deceive and lead them astray.[9]

But the restoration of the gospel changed that. President Jedediah M. Grant pointed out,

> When the Priesthood of God is upon the earth, then the priesthood of the devil may be seen operating for he has got one. When the kingdom of God is on the earth, you may expect to see a special display or manifestation of the opposite to the Gospel of the kingdom, or the Priesthood of God.[10]

There are then two opposing priesthoods on the earth, but Satan's is far inferior to God's. He is understandably very defensive about this issue. Elder Charles S. Hyde, president of the Netherlands Mission, shared this experience in general conference:

> We had one in the mission field afflicted with an evil spirit. . . . I came into the room upon one occasion, and the evil spirit sprang upon me and seized me by the throat with a grip of iron. . . . He shouted with a voice that was most terrific. He declared himself to be the devil. "My name is Satan," he declared, "and I have more authority than you." And again tightening his grip upon my throat, he declared, "I have more authority than you." I could not speak, but I looked the person in the eye, and [then] releasing his grip and falling upon the bed, that same voice declared, "No, I have not more authority," and he hid his face in the pillow and was subject to the power of the Priesthood. Elder Kooyman . . . anointed him with oil, and with other elders I laid my hands upon him, and I began to confirm the anointing. When I reached the point in prayer, that "in the name of Jesus Christ," I was going to say,

"we rebuke the spirit," he sprang from the bed, and pleaded: "Do not use that name. . . ." We placed him upon the bed, and in the name of Jesus Christ I rebuked that spirit and commanded it to depart from him, and the person who was afflicted fell limp upon the bed and slept for hours, the first peaceful sleep he had enjoyed for several days."[11]

The history of the restored Church is replete with displays of Satan's latter-day handiwork.

Joseph Smith's encounter with the powers of darkness in the Sacred Grove was a dramatic introduction to Satan's labors to counterfeit and destroy. The adversary continued his efforts to deceive throughout the opening years of this dispensation, stirring up the hearts of men in opposition to the work and sending false manifestations to imitate the revelations of God.

Less than a month after the organization of the Church, Joseph visited Colesville, in southern New York, where he taught the principles of the gospel to his friend, Newel Knight. He challenged Brother Knight to pray; however, Newel declined. The next morning, depressed and self-reproaching, Knight went to the woods to commune with heaven. However, he found himself stifled in mind and spirit, incapable of uttering a word.

He returned to his house, visibly agitated and weighed down with depression, and asked his wife to send for the Prophet. When Joseph arrived, Brother Knight's face was distorted and his limbs "twisted in every shape and appearance possible to imagine."[12] Finally some unseen power lifted him off the floor and began to toss him about the room. The news of the commotion quickly spread until a small crowd of neighbors had gathered to witness the horrible scene.

Joseph writes of the incident,

I succeeded in getting hold of him by the hand, when almost immediately he spoke to me, and with great earnestness requested me to cast the devil out of him, saying that he knew he was in him, and that he also knew that I could cast him out.

I replied, "If you know that I can, it shall be done;" and then almost unconsciously I rebuked the devil, and commanded him in the name of Jesus Christ to depart from him; when immediately Newel spoke out and said that he saw the devil leave him and vanish from his sight. This was the first miracle which was done in the Church, or by any member of it; and it was done not by man, nor by the power of man, but it was done by God, and by the power of godliness; therefore let the honor and the praise, the dominion and the glory, be ascribed to the Father, Son, and Holy Spirit, for ever and ever. Amen.[13]

Another challenge from the adversary, though of a different character, occurred only a few months later. Following a stay in Colesville, the Prophet returned to Fayette, New York, to find that "Satan had been lying in wait to deceive, and seeking whom he might devour."

Brother Hiram Page had in his possession a certain stone, by which he had obtained certain "revelations" . . . all of which were entirely at variance with the order of God's house.[14]

These were *real* revelations, given by miraculous means and, by every appearance, genuine communications from God. Many prominent members of the new church, including Oliver Cowdery, wholeheartedly believed in the messages brought forth by this instrument of magic. The issue of Hiram Page's "seer stone" became a source of contention, resentment, and confusion. Desiring a resolution on the matter, Joseph sought the word of the Lord.

The response was Doctrine and Covenants 28, in which the Lord responded,

Behold, verily, verily, I say unto thee, no one shall be appointed to receive commandments and revelations in this Church excepting my servant Joseph Smith, Jun., for he receiveth them even as Moses.

And thou shalt be obedient unto the things which I shall give unto him, . . . to declare faithfully the commandments and the revelations, with power and authority unto the church. (D&C 28:2–3)

One remarkable aspect of the seer stone incident is found in the counsel the Lord gave to Oliver Cowdery—advising him to deal confidentially with Hiram Page. God doesn't want to publicly humiliate any of us. He is always sensitive to our feelings:

And again, thou shalt take thy brother, Hiram Page, between him and thee alone, and tell him that those things which he hath written from that stone are not of me and that Satan deceiveth him. (D&C 28:11)

The Prophet writes that in response to this firm but gentle rebuke, Brother Page and all those who had accepted his revelations renounced them and that, thanks to the Lord's intervention, the entire issue was settled "much to our mutual satisfaction and happiness."

False prophets and demonic activities continued to pepper the pages of early Church history. Kirtland, Ohio, in particular, was a hotbed of convincing satanic manifestations.

The Prophet writes,

> Soon after the Gospel was established in Kirtland, and during the absence of the authorities of the Church, many false spirits were introduced, many strange visions were seen, and wild, enthusiastic notions were entertained; men ran out of doors under the influence of this spirit, and some of them got upon the stumps of trees and shouted, and all kinds of extravagances were entered into by them.[15]

If we did not understand the diabolical nature of these manifestations, they would be almost comical. But these violent fits of jumping and screaming were no laughing matter. Such displays were, and are still, Satan's efforts to bring disgrace upon the kingdom of God.

In one such instance, Joseph ordained Harvey Whitlock to the office of high priest. No sooner was the ordination performed than Brother Whitlock

> turned as black as Lyman [Wight] was white. His fingers were set like claws. He went around the room and showed his hands and tried to speak. His eyes were in the shape of oval O's. . . .
>
> Joseph bowed his head, and in a short time got up and commanded Satan to leave Harvey, laying his hands upon his head at the same time.
>
> At that very instant an old man said to weigh two hundred and fourteen pounds, sitting in the window, turned a complete summersault in the house and came down with his back across a bench, and lay helpless.
>
> Joseph told Lyman to cast Satan out. He did. . . . The evil spirit left him, and as quick as lightning Harvey Green fell bound and screamed like a panther. Satan was cast out of him, but immediately entered someone else. This continued all day and the greater part of the night."[16]

Repeating the pattern he had introduced in New York, Satan also poured forth a fresh flurry of false revelations during the early Kirtland period. A woman named Hubbel made a convincing pretense as a prophetess and deceived many of the Saints. Another would-be prophet, a former slave generally known as Black Pete, claimed the

Stephen J. Stirling

regular visitation of angels who gave him revelations in the form of letters from heaven. On one occasion, according to President George A. Smith,

> Black Pete got sight of one of those revelations carried by a black angel, he started after it, and ran off a steep wash bank twenty-five feet high, passed through a tree top into the Chagrin River beneath. He came out with a few scratches, and his ardor somewhat cooled.[17]

We have to smile as we read about some of Satan's antics to get attention here on earth. But ultimately, the activities of the adversary and his followers are no laughing matter. I repeat, his power is something to be taken seriously.

## Notes

1. Joseph Fielding Smith, *Answers to Gospel Questions* (Salt Lake City: Deseret Book Company, 1957), 1:178.

2. Brigham Young, in *Journal of Discourses* (London: Latter-day Saints' Book Depot, 1854–86), 4:133.

3. James E. Talmage, *Articles of Faith* (Salt Lake City: Deseret News, 1899), 63. (Italics added.)

4. Ibid.

5. Margie Calhoun, *Stories of Insight and Inspiration* (Salt Lake City: Bountiful Press, 1993), 272–73.

6. Ibid., 273–74.

7. Joseph Smith, *History of the Church of Jesus Christ of Latter-day Saints*, 6 vols., ed. B. H. Roberts, 2nd ed. rev. (Salt Lake City: Deseret Book, 1927), 4:576.

8. Brigham Young, *Discourses of Brigham Young,* comp. John A. Widtsoe (Salt Lake City: Deseret Book Company, 1925), 68.

9. Orson Pratt, in *Journal of Discourses*, 13:68. (Italics added.)

10. Jedediah M. Grant, in *Journal of Discourses*, 2:11.

11. Charles S. Hyde, in Conference Report, April 1926, 125.

12. Joseph Smith, *History of the Church of Jesus Christ of Latter-day Saints*, 1:82.

13. Ibid., 1:82–83.

14. Ibid., 1:109–110.

15. Ibid., 4:580.

16. Hyrum L. Andrus and Helen Mae Andrus, *They Knew the Prophet* (Salt Lake City: Bookcraft Inc., 1974), 17–18.

17. George A. Smith, in *Journal of Discourses,* 11:4.

# 7

# THE FORCES OF LIGHT

The real power of the universe, however, is in the hands of God. Anything else is counterfeit—a cheap imitation. That is why our Heavenly Father will never allow demonstrations of Satan's power to go unanswered. The world ultimately needs to understand that God reigns. This is not a matter of pride. It is simply an issue of a loving Father protecting his children. The Lord's response to the maelstrom of spiritual darkness in early Church history, and today, is Doctrine and Covenants 50. This revelation provides the key to identifying false as well as true messengers:

> Behold, verily I say unto you, that there are many spirits which are false spirits, which have gone forth in the earth, deceiving the world.
> And also Satan hath sought to deceive you, that he might overthrow you. (D&C 50:2–3)[1]

Unfortunately, Satan also employs mortal accomplices in the work of darkness. These people occupy positions of power and influence. They can be public officials, celebrities, star athletes, professors of education, or news media personalities. But they may also be friends and associates with whom we rub shoulders every day.

> Behold, verily I say unto you, there are hypocrites among you, who have deceived some, which has given the adversary power; . . .
> But the hypocrites shall be detected and shall be cut off, either in life or in death, even as I will. (D&C 50:7–8)

These warnings are then followed by a challenge to seek the Holy Ghost, to preach by the inspiration of the Comforter, and to receive the word by the Spirit of truth. The goal of this striving is to give light to our souls—to edify.

> And that which doth not edify is not of God, and is darkness.
> That which is of God is light; and he that receiveth light, and continueth in God, receiveth more light; and that light groweth brighter and brighter until the perfect day. (D&C 50:23–24)

It's all about receiving light—and light is what allows us to find our way amidst the darkness.

> And again, verily I say unto you, and I say it that you may know the truth, that you may chase darkness from among you. (D&C 50:25)

God provides us with the power to identify and to dispel the darkness:

> Wherefore . . . if you behold a spirit manifested that you cannot understand, and you receive not that spirit, ye shall ask of the Father in the name of Jesus; and if he give not unto you that spirit, then you may know that it is not of God.
> And it shall be given unto you, power over that spirit; and you shall proclaim against that spirit with a loud voice that it is not of God. (D&C 50:31–32)

This instruction to cast out evil comes with an added caution, however. The spirit of darkness must be rebuked in a spirit of light:

> Not with railing accusation, that ye be not overcome, neither with boasting nor rejoicing, lest you be seized therewith. . . .
> And by giving heed and doing these things which ye have received, and which ye shall hereafter receive—and the kingdom is given you of the Father, and power to overcome all things which are not ordained of him. (D&C 50:33, 35)

The Lord is very specific in warning us against "railing accusation" as well as "boasting or rejoicing." Satan deceives with rage, violence, and flattery in the hearts of men. But we cannot oppose him utilizing the same weapons of mass destruction. The priesthood must operate from a stance of righteousness and humility.

No power or influence can or ought to be maintained by virtue of the priesthood, only by persuasion, by long-suffering, by gentleness and meekness, and by love unfeigned;

By kindness, and by pure knowledge, which shall greatly enlarge the soul without hypocrisy and without guile. (D&C 121:41–42)

It becomes clear, then, that you and I have to operate by a completely different set of rules. We have to play nice. We aren't allowed to hit below the belt, kick, use the rabbit punch, or throw sand in our opponent's eyes while Satan can (and does) employ all those unsportsmanlike tactics. He cheats and we can't. That seems unfair to the carnal mind, until we realize that in playing by God's rules we will always win.

Missionary Robert Nixon records how he learned this lesson. He had been asked to give a priesthood blessing. But upon entering the room where the blessing was to be performed, he encountered an "evil force" which overcame him suddenly. He felt ill and began to shake uncontrollably. He excused himself and stepped alone into another room, but the condition grew more severe. "[He] realized that an evil spirit was actually within [him]."

> I locked the door and knelt down. As I started to pray vocally, I found that I couldn't speak. . . . I began to pray silently, and as I did, the shaking seized me so violently that it was difficult for me to remain on my knees.
>
> [All of this sounds very familiar. Elder Nixon continues.]
>
> I strained physically to regain the use of my voice to call upon the Lord, but when I did, it didn't sound like my voice. But, knowing that I held the priesthood, I commanded the evil spirit to leave me. [However] *it did not leave!* . . .
>
> Again I commanded it to depart, and was almost seized with panic as I realized that it still remained within me. . . .
>
> I humbled myself and continued to pray in all earnestness. In doing so, the thought came to me that when I had previously commanded the adversary, I had commanded with arrogance instead of humility.
>
> Being aware of this, the third time I commanded the evil power to leave, I did so gently and humbly, in a soft voice, and it began to depart. . . . Finally, the evil influence was gone . . . leaving me physically exhausted. All was replaced by the comforting, warm glow of the Spirit of the Lord. . . .

This was not only a frightening and literally painful encounter with the adversary, but also a valuable lesson to have learned; the power of the priesthood can operate only when called upon with authority, faith, *and* humility.[2]

Authority, faith, and humility are key qualities we must possess when dealing with the adversary. We cannot confront the powers of darkness with bombast and arrogance. We cannot take the Lord's patronage for granted. It is not enough to take refuge in our possession of the priesthood or the prideful assurance that God *must* be on our side. That kind of "We're Number One" attitude alienates us from Him. Power over darkness requires us to stay in the light.

On one of his missions, President Wilford Woodruff visited a hall where spiritualist meetings were regularly held. He had prepared for his attendance there, specifically praying to his Heavenly Father to neutralize the influence of the medium who was in charge.

> An audience of about three hundred people had assembled, and the medium was prepared to give his lecture and his spiritualistic demonstration, as he had been doing on former occasions; but he found it impossible to proceed with the usual manifestations. He jumped down from the platform, walked around through the aisles, here and there among the audience, and finally came to Brother Woodruff. Shaking his fist in Brother Woodruff's face, he said: "You are the man who is keeping me from doing anything tonight!"
>
> Brother Woodruff said: "Yes, I am the fellow. I am here with the priesthood of the Living God, and I have rebuked the power of the adversary. You can't do anything while I am here!"
>
> After a while the audience asked Brother Woodruff to please withdraw, and he did so; and they had the devil's own time after he left.[3]

The priesthood of God is our sure defense against the dark side. But the prayer of faith from the fountain of a righteous heart can be just as effective a weapon against the mechanizations of Satan. President Heber J. Grant recounted this incident from his boyhood involving one of the dark side's favorite playthings—the Ouija board.

Also known as a spirit board, a talking board, or a "conversation with dead people" board, the Ouija (pronounced *wee-ja* or *wee-jee*) board is a popular instrument of the occult. According to the manufacturers, the board allows its users to "communicate with spirits from the unseen world," offering hours and hours of satanic fun! The surface of the board is decorated with the letters of the alphabet, the numbers 0 to 9, and the words *yes* and *no*. With the aid of a pointer, the occupants of the spirit realm painstakingly piece together the numbers and letters to answer questions and relay personal messages to the world of the living.

Marketed internationally by a popular game company, the Ouija board is considered party entertainment and may even be found on the shelves of Toys "R" Us. However, a spirit board is not and never has been a toy. Modern prophets have universally identified Ouija boards as tools of darkness and have counseled the Saints to avoid them.

President Grant relates,

> I happened to be in what is known as the Octagon House. . . . The old building still stands there. I was a young boy at the time and my mother [Rachel Ivins Grant] was then going out sewing by the day to earn her livelihood. . . . While we were sitting in the little sewing room mother was requested to go into the parlor where the people were laughing and joking over the messages they were receiving from a planchette [a Ouija board] which was operating on the table. My mother positively refused to go into the room, or have anything to do with a message received on the planchette, stating that "Brother Brigham" had announced that the people should leave planchettes alone. . . . She further stated that if you followed the planchette around through the city you would discover that it had left a trail of apostasy behind, especially if people paid any attention to the messages. . . .
>
> Finally they laughingly said that if she would not go where the planchette was they would bring it where she was, and they brought it into the room where my mother was sewing. She refused to look at it, and they could not make it work in that room where she was. It simply would not deliver any messages there. They went back into the parlor, where it worked splendidly, and they continued their laughing and joking. They soon came back and asked my mother to come into the parlor; and very much to my astonishment she went into the parlor, notwithstanding she had said she would not go where it was.
>
> As soon as she entered the parlor, the planchette would not work, and they were unable to make it move as long as she remained in the room. When we got home that night, I said: "Mother, why did you go in the parlor where the planchette was when you said Brother Brigham

had advised people to keep away from it?" She said, "My boy, when they came into the little room where I was sewing, and brought the planchette, I prayed to the Lord that it might not have power to work in my presence; I told the Lord that I had not gone where it was, and now that they had brought it where I was, I rebuked its power to work and it could not move. . . . When they afterwards asked me to go into the parlor, I again prayed to the Lord to give me the impression that I could stop the thing from working, and that if he would give me that impression I would go into the parlor. . . . The impression came to me that it could not move about in my presence, so I went in the parlor, and as you know, they could not make it work while I was there."[4]

The adversary can manifest himself in many ways, but those with the Spirit are promised the ability to distinguish light from darkness. Faithful men and women are also given power over Satan's devices. Whatever form this deceit may take, Heavenly Father will support us when we walk in the light.

## The Hosts of Satan

So "Satan is abroad in the land" (D&C 52:14) and the power of the priesthood and personal righteousness are in place to counter him. It is then reasonable to expect the adversary to bring in reinforcements whenever necessary. And he *does* have the "manpower."

In an instance referred to earlier, the Savior visited the shores of the Gadarenes where he encountered "a man with an unclean spirit" (Mark 5:2) whom no one could bind or tame.

> But when he saw Jesus afar off, he ran and worshipped him,
> And cried with a loud voice, and said, *What have I to do with thee, Jesus, thou Son of the most high God?* I adjure thee by God, that thou torture me not. (Mark 5:6–7; italics added)

It is interesting that Satan and his hosts could so easily recognize Jesus as the Son of God. That is because they have no veil of forgetfulness over their minds as mortals do. They remember the premortal world, they remember us, and they remember the gifts, talents, and missions that were assigned to all of us. They remember you! The ability of evil spirits to know what you and I have forgotten is an advantage in their favor. With that advantage they attempt to lead us astray at every opportunity in order to prevent us from fulfilling our foreordained missions.

That is the reason it is so imperative for each and every one of us to study the scriptures, follow the counsel of the prophets, and become intimately acquainted with the details, warnings, and promises in our patriarchal blessings. Divine revelation from these sources nullifies any advantage of advance intelligence possessed by the agents of the dark side.

As for the nature and identity of those agents,

> And he [Jesus] asked him, What is thy name? And he answered, saying, *My name is Legion: for we are many.*
>
> And he besought him much that he would not send him away out of the country.
>
> Now there was there nigh unto the mountains a great herd of swine feeding.
>
> And *all the devils* besought him, saying, Send us into the swine, that we may enter into them.
>
> And forthwith Jesus gave them leave. And the unclean spirits went out, and entered into the swine: and the herd ran violently down a steep place into the sea, (*they were about two thousand;*) and they were choked in the sea." (Mark 5: 9–13; italics added)

Yes, Satan definitely has the reserves (by the thousands or even millions) to throw into the battle. And occasionally that is enough to temporarily turn the tide in his favor.

Years ago Apostle Marriner W. Merrill, who was then serving as the president of the Logan Utah Temple, related this remarkable incident:

> [Brother Merrill] was sitting in his office one morning, he said, when he noticed from the window a company of people coming up the hill to the Temple. As they entered the Temple grounds they presented rather a strange appearance. . . .
>
> A little later a person unknown to Brother Merrill entered the room. Brother Merrill said to him: "Who are you and who are these people who have come up and taken possession of the Temple grounds unannounced?" He [The man] answered and said: "I am Satan and these are my people." Brother Merrill then said: "What do you want? Why have you come here?" Satan replied: "I don't like the work that is going on in this Temple and feel that it should be discontinued. Will you stop it?" Brother Merrill answered and said emphatically, "No, we will not stop it. The work must go on." "Since you refuse to stop it, I

will tell you what I propose to do," the adversary said. "I will take these people, my followers, and distribute them throughout this Temple district, and will instruct them to whisper in the ears of people, persuading them not to go to the Temple, and thus bring about the cessation of your Temple work." Satan then withdrew. . . .

For quite a period of time the spirit of indifference to Temple work seemed to take possession of the people and very few came to the House of the Lord.[5]

One of the most terrifying displays of Satan's reality was described by President Heber C. Kimball as he told of introducing the gospel in Great Britain. It was on the eve of the first baptisms in Preston, England:

Sunday, July 30th (1837), about daybreak, Elder Isaac Russell . . . came up to the third story, where Elder Hyde and myself were sleeping, and called out, "Brother Kimball, I want you should get up and pray for me that I may be delivered from the evil spirits that are tormenting me to such a degree that I feel I cannot live long unless I obtain relief."

. . . [We] immediately arose . . . and we laid hands on him, I being mouth, and prayed that the Lord would have mercy on him, and rebuked the devil.

While thus engaged, I was struck with great force by some invisible power, and fell senseless on the floor. . . . Elder Hyde and Richards then assisted me to get on the bed, but my agony was so great I could not endure it, and I . . . bowed my knees and prayed. I then arose and sat up on the bed, when a vision was opened to our minds, and we could distinctly see the evil spirits, who foamed and gnashed their teeth at us. We gazed upon them about an hour and a half. . . . Space appeared before us, and we saw the devils coming in legions, with their leaders, who came within a few feet of us. They came towards us like armies rushing to battle. They appeared to be men of full stature, possessing every form and feature of men in the flesh, who were angry and desperate; and I shall never forget the vindictive malignity depicted on their countenances as they looked me in the eye.[6]

On another occasion, he spoke of the demons:

I saw their hands, their eyes, and every feature of their faces, the hair on their heads and their ears, in short they had full-formed bodies.[7]

I perspired exceedingly, my clothes becoming as wet as if I had been taken out of the river. I felt excessive pain, and was in the greatest distress for some time. . . . We distinctly heard those spirits talk and express their wrath and hellish designs against us. However, the Lord delivered us from them, and blessed us exceedingly that day.[8]

Later, Elder Kimball narrated his experience in Preston to the Prophet Joseph Smith and asked him frankly if he had done anything wrong that he "should have such a manifestation."

"No, Brother Heber," he replied, "at that time you were nigh unto the Lord; there was only a thin veil between you and Him, but you could not see Him. When I heard of it, it gave me great joy, for I then knew that the work of God had taken root in that land. It was this that caused the devil to make a struggle to kill you."

Joseph then related some of his own experience, in many contests he had had with the evil one, and said: "The nearer a person approaches the Lord, a greater power will be manifested by the adversary to prevent the accomplishment of His purposes."[9]

President Hugh B. Brown provides us with a more intimate example of this same principle. In the fall of 1953, Brother Brown's prospects were promising. A prominent lawyer-businessman in Edmonton, Alberta, Canada, he had been making efforts to establish himself in the petroleum industry. Now, on the eve of his seventieth birthday, his dreams of success and fortune were so close he could taste them. But then a discomfort began to quietly trouble him—"a feeling of uncertainty" and "unfulfilled destiny."[10]

Unable to be at peace with these feelings in his heart, one October morning he "went into the mountains and talked to the Lord in prayer."

I told Him that although it looked like I was going to become wealthy as a result of my oil ventures, if in His wisdom it would not be good for me or my family I hoped He would not permit it to come to pass.

That night I drove from the camp at Rocky Mountain House down to Edmonton still spiritually disturbed and depressed. Without having dinner that night, I went into the bedroom by myself, told my wife that she should stay in the other room as I felt I would not have a good night's rest. All night long I wrestled with the evil spirit. I was possessed with the spirit of wishing that I could be rubbed out of existence. I had no thought of suicide, but wished the Lord would provide a way for me to cease to be. The room was full of darkness, and an evil spirit prevailed, so real that I was almost consumed by it. About three A.M. I was barely able to call to my wife. She came in and asked what was the matter. Upon closing the door, she said, "Oh Hugh! What is in this room?" And I replied, "The Devil." We spent the balance of the night together, much of it on our knees. The next morning upon going to the office . . . I knelt in prayer again and asked for deliverance from the evil spirit. I felt a peaceful spirit come over me and phoned my wife to that effect.

That night, while I was taking a bath about ten o'clock, the telephone rang and she [my wife] called me and said, "Salt Lake City is calling."

Upon going to the phone, I heard a voice which said, "This is David O. McKay calling. The Lord wants you to spend the balance of your life in the service of the Church. The Council of the Twelve have just voted that you should . . . become an Assistant to the Twelve."[11]

As we have seen before, Satan likes to be in attendance for special occasions. Whenever possible, he will be on hand to bring a dark cloud over those events that will further God's kingdom and seriously undermine his own. Know that opposition from the dark side can often be a sign that God is preparing you for great things.

Of our enemies beyond the veil, Brigham Young taught,

The invisible spirits are active. And every person who desires and strives to be a Saint is closely watched by fallen spirits that came here when Lucifer fell, and by the *spirits of wicked persons who have been here in tabernacles and departed from them*, but who are still under the control of the prince of the power of the air."[12]

(So there *are* such things as ghosts.) President Young continues.

And you will learn that they are striving with all their might—labouring and toiling diligently as any individual would to accomplish an act in this world—to destroy the children of men.[13]

Brigham Young also verified the magnitude of these legions as every bit the "armies rushing to battle" that Heber C. Kimball described them to be.

There are millions and millions of spirits in these valleys, both good and evil. We are surrounded with more evil spirits than good ones . . . The spirits that were cast out of heaven . . . have been here all the time.[14]

Well could President Kimball speak from personal experience regarding Satan's reality, his power, and the sheer number of his forces.

And yet, with his warning, he also offered encouragement:

> After all this some persons will say to me, that there are no evil spirits. I
> tell you they are thicker than the "Mormons" are in this country, but the
> Lord has said that there are more for us than there can be against us.[15]

If indeed, "We are surrounded with more evil spirits than good
ones," how then can there be "more for us than there can be against
us"? That seeming contradiction is reconciled in the simple reality that
the forces of eternity stand prepared at a moment's notice to come to
our rescue. But they will generally not be deployed unless we request
additional troops. As mentioned previously, neither the Father nor his
angels "hover" (get it? *angels . . . hover*), like meddlesome nursemaids
over our lives. To do so would jeopardize agency. God holds his mas-
sive army in reserve, willing and ready to respond instantly to our
needs and defense. All that is required of us is to ask for help.

However, statements of the brethren regarding the numerical
strength of Satan's forces are critical reminders to all of us. We are
a generation living in a wicked world, seemingly surrounded by the
armies of evil.

Elisha, the prophet in Israel, lived in the same kind of overwhelm-
ingly wicked world. He preached to a people struggling with sin and
apostasy, ruled by an unrighteous monarch. But the immediate threat
to Israel's peace was their pagan enemy to the north, Syria.

Now, on several occasions, the king of Syria had attacked Israel,
only to have his battle plans thwarted by the intervention of Elisha,
who knew his every move by revelation. This had to be stopped. So the
king sent his army to locate and capture Israel's prophet.

> And he [the king] said, Go and spy where he is, that I may send and
> fetch him. . . .
> Therefore sent he thither horses, and chariots, and a great host: and
> they came by night, and compassed the city about.
> And when the servant of the man of God was risen early, and gone
> forth, behold, an host compassed the city both with horses and chari-
> ots. And his servant said unto him [Elisha], Alas, my master! how shall
> we do? (2 Kings 6:13–15)

This question is the equivalent of, "Sir, I believe we're in trouble."
And by any analysis, the situation did look rather bleak. There they

stood, defenseless and trapped, surrounded by a seemingly innumerable and vastly powerful army. Our condition, as Saints in the midst of Babylon, is certainly similar. How often do we consider the dismal odds working against us, in favor of wickedness, and ask ourselves in despair, "How shall we do?" The prophets never get discouraged. Then and now their response to the righteous is always optimistic.

> And he [Elisha] answered, *Fear not: for they that be with us are more than they that be with them.*
>
> And Elisha prayed, and said, Lord, I pray thee, open his eyes, that he may see. And the Lord opened the eyes of the young man; and he saw: and, behold, the mountain was full of horses and chariots of fire round about Elisha. (2 Kings 6:16–17; italics added)

This heavenly host of glory far outnumbered and outgunned the paltry army of Syria. The outcome was symbolic of our lives in the fight of good against evil.

> And when they came down to him, Elisha prayed unto the Lord, and said, Smite this people, I pray thee, with blindness. And he smote them [the army] with blindness according to the word of Elisha. (2 Kings 6:18)

There is indeed a battle raging all around us, and it may seem, at times, that we are encircled and hopelessly outnumbered. But there are powers unseen and forces undetected that stand in our defense. They are prepared and anxious to come to our aid in this great warfare for our souls and the souls of men. "Fear not: for they that be with us are more than they that be with them."

## Notes

1. Of false spirits and false revelations, Brigham Young had this to add.

 "It was revealed to me that if this people did not receive the spirit of revelation that God had sent for the salvation of the world, they would receive false spirits, and would have revelation. Men would have revelation, women would have revelation, the priest in the pulpit and the deacon under the pulpit, would have revelation, and the people would have revelation enough to damn the whole nation, and nations of them, unless they would hearken to the voice of God." (Brigham Young, in *Journal of Discourses* [London: Latter-day Saints' Book Depot, 1854–86], 13:280–81.)

2. Margie Calhoun, *When Faith Writes the Story* (Salt Lake City: Bountiful Press, 1993), 234–36. (Italics added.)

3. Margie Calhoun, *Stories of Insight and Inspiration* (Salt Lake City: Bountiful Press, 1993), 275.

4. Heber J. Grant, "The Planchette or Ouija Board." *The Relief Society Magazine*, Jan. 1920, 73–74.

A continuation of the cited article is instructive:

"In connection with this story it is related by our First Counsellor Clarissa Smith Williams, that some one presented to her children some years since, an Ouija board for a Christmas present. She paid little attention to it until one of the little boys placed the thing on the table, as he had seen others do, and put his little hands upon it. It commenced to move at once, and so terrible was the influence which accompanied it that the child began screaming, and was almost convulsed with terror and distress. Sister Williams at once took the board and threw it into the fire, and no such thing has entered her home since. What about your homes, dear friends, and what about your children?" (75)

5. N.B. Lundwall, *Temples of the Most High* (Salt Lake City: Bookcraft, 1952), 99.

6. Orson F. Whitney, *Life of Heber C. Kimball* (Salt Lake City: Stevens & Wallace, Inc., 1945), 129–30.

7. Heber C. Kimball, in *Journal of Discourses,* 3:229.

8. Whitney, *Life of Heber C. Kimball,* 130–32.

9. Ibid. (Italics added.)

10. Eugene E. Campbell and Richard D. Poll, *Hugh B. Brown—His Life and Thought* (Salt Lake City: Bookcraft, 1975), 218.

11. Ibid., 218–19.

12. Brigham Young, in *Journal of Discourses* (London: Latter-day Saints' Book Depot, 1854–86), 7:239. (Italics added.)

With regards to ghosts as we traditionally understand them, Brigham Young also had this to say when addressing those who give heed to false spirits:

"This is the difference. We receive revelation from Heaven, you receive your revelations from every *foul spirit that has departed this life*, and gone out of the bodies of mobbers, murderers, highwaymen, drunkards, thieves, liars, and every kind of debauched character, whose spirits are floating around here, and searching and seeking whom they can destroy; for they are the servants of the devil, and they are permitted to come now to reveal to the people." (13:281; italics added)

13. Ibid., 7:239.

14. Ibid., 4:133.

15. Ibid., 3:230.

# 8

# THE DECISIVE CLASH OF
# GOOD AND EVIL

So, here we are in the midst of a great conflict, and a final dramatic confrontation is fast approaching. None of this is breaking news to the Saints. The Lord revealed the growth of Satan's power in the opening pages of the Doctrine and Covenants:

> The hour is not yet, but is nigh at hand, when peace shall be taken from the earth, and the devil shall have power over his own dominion. (D&C 1:35)

In August 1831, Joseph Smith and his brethren traveled to Missouri to consecrate the land of Zion as a gathering place for the Saints. There at McIlwaine's Bend on the Missouri River, Elder William W. Phelps saw the destroyer in an open vision, riding upon the waters in power and majesty. Others heard the noise, but did not see the vision. (Doctrine and Covenants 61, headnote and DHC I:203.) The demonstration seemed to be a kind of calling card to announce Satan's intentions of destruction to the Saints of this dispensation.

President Joseph Fielding Smith comments,

> Satan has control now. No matter where you look, he is in control, even in our own land. He is guiding the governments as far as the Lord will permit him. That is why there is so much strife, turmoil, and confusion all over the earth. One master mind is governing the nations. It is not the President of the United States; . . . it is not the king or government of England or any other land; it is Satan himself.[1]

In possession of such power and influence, Satan is dangerous beyond our imagination. Driven by deranged ambition and bent on the destruction of humanity, he is, by any standard, insane—a psychopath, like Nero, Stalin, Hitler, or any of history's cruelest megalomaniacs. Our most sacred liturgy attests to his deluded assurance of control with the declaration, "This is the great day of my power"—a power that has no inhibitions and knows no geographical or political boundaries.

But the Lord himself stands in his way. He has, in our day, reestablished and prepared his kingdom on earth to stand in opposition to the demented forces of evil. We are the army of Jehovah. In the coming battle, each of us has a mission to fulfill.

President Ezra Taft Benson told the youth of Zion,

> Make no mistake about it—you are a marked generation. There has never been more expected of the faithful in such a short period of time than there is of us. Never before on the face of the earth have the forces of evil and the forces of good been so well organized. Now is the great day of the devil's power. But now is also the great day of the Lord's power. . . .
>
> Each day the forces of evil and the forces of good enlist new recruits. Each day we personally make many decisions showing the cause we support. The final outcome is certain—the forces of righteousness will finally win. But what remains to be seen is where each of us personally, now and in the future, will stand in this battle—and how tall we will stand. Will we be true to our last days and fulfill our foreordained missions?[2]

In the final analysis, our performance in the latter days has already been foreshadowed by our premortal training and our performance in the War in Heaven. Referring to our former victory over Satan in the spirit world, Elder James J. Hamula of the Seventy taught,

> Understand, my young friends, that there is only one way to win the war against Satan, and that is to win it in the same way it was won in the beginning. . . .
>
> Satan was overcome in the beginning by (1) *faith* in the Lord Jesus Christ and His atoning sacrifice, (2) *testimony* of Him that was steadfastly kept to the very end, and (3) *consecration* of oneself to the Lord and His work. If this was the means for defeating him in the beginning, you can be sure that this is the one sure way to defeat him now.[3]

Drawing upon obedience to the commandments and personal righteousness, Heavenly Father promises us in the Doctrine and Covenants at least six times that by doing so, "the gates of hell shall not prevail against you." Please note the promise of this prophetic imagery—that Satan and his hosts will be on the defensive. Gates traditionally don't assail anyone. We, the army of righteousness, will be marching on the offensive against the fortress of evil. In spite of overwhelming numbers and the frightening power possessed by the dark side, Satan's hosts will ultimately cower before the might of righteousness—a simple combination of virtuous living, intelligence, the gifts of the Spirit, and godly authority.

Joseph Smith said it this way:

> Who can drag into daylight and develop the hidden mysteries of the false spirits that so frequently are made manifest among the Latter-day Saints? We answer that no man can do this without *the Priesthood*, and having *a knowledge* of the laws by which spirits are governed; for no man knows the things of God, but by the Spirit of God.[4]

President James E. Faust reaffirmed our capability to claim this power through keeping the commandments and a commitment to sacred priesthood covenants.

> All who come unto Christ by obedience to the covenants and ordinances of the gospel can thwart Satan's efforts. The humble followers of the divine Master need not be deceived by the devil if they will be honest and true to their fellow men and women, go to the house of the Lord, receive the sacrament worthily, observe the Sabbath day, pay their tithes and offerings, offer contrite prayers, engage in the Lord's work, and follow those who preside over them.
>
> There are forces that will save us from the ever increasing lying, disorder, violence, chaos, destruction, misery, and deceit that are upon the earth. Those saving forces are the everlasting principles, covenants, and ordinances of the eternal gospel of the Lord Jesus Christ. These same principles, covenants, and ordinances are coupled with the rights and powers of the priesthood of Almighty God.[5]

Ours is *a personal war against Satan*! We all, individually, march in the footsteps of the great Captain Moroni. He was obliged (reluctantly) to wage a war which he did not begin, but one which he was determined to finish, because there was so much at stake. Consider

Mormon's inspired tribute to him. It needs to be a description that fits all of us.

> And Moroni was a strong and a mighty man; he was a man of a perfect understanding; yea, a man that did not delight in bloodshed; a man whose soul did joy in the liberty and the freedom of his country, and his brethren from bondage and slavery;
>
> Yea, a man whose heart did swell with thanksgiving to his God, for the many privileges and blessings which he bestowed upon his people; a man who did labor for the welfare and safety of his people.
>
> Yea, and he was a man who was firm in the faith of Christ, and he had sworn with an oath to defend his people, his rights, and his country, and his religion, even to the loss of his blood.
>
> . . . And this was the faith of Moroni, and his heart did glory in it; not in the shedding of blood, but in doing good, in preserving his people, yea, in keeping the commandments of God, yea, and resisting iniquity.
>
> *Yea, verily, verily I say unto you, if all men had been, and were, and ever would be, like unto Moroni, behold, the very powers of hell would have been shaken forever; yea, the devil would never have power over the hearts of the children of men.* (Alma 48:11–13, 16–17; italics added)

Captain Moroni, by his very nature, heaped measurable grief upon Satan's already miserable existence. Every morning, when Moroni got out of bed, there was an audible moan that echoed through the halls of hell. "Oh, no. He's awake again." In our personal campaign against the dark side, each of us needs to dedicate our lives to making Satan's life just that wretched.

You need to conduct your life in such a way that each day as you arise, you may imagine the adversary hissing through gritted teeth, "Oh, no. He's (or she's) awake again." If you ever *must* think of Satan, picture him, somewhere in his shadowed realm, clinching his eyes shut in painful realization that his work of destruction is going to be that much more difficult because of you.

Many years ago, President Thomas S. Monson said,

> Today we are encamped against the greatest array of sin, vice, and evil ever assembled before our eyes. Such formidable enemies may cause lesser hearts to shrink or shun the fight. . . . [As] we do battle against him who would thwart the purposes of God, . . . I pray that each of us will stand in his or her appointed place, that the battle for the souls of men will indeed be won.[6]

# Millennium—Temporary End of the Conflict

In the meantime, Satan's time is running out. Elder Joseph Fielding Smith has said,

> Satan has had sway. He has usurped authority and found favor with men. . . .
>
> But this condition . . . is drawing to its close. The day is near at hand when this earth itself will be changed, when righteousness shall prevail, and wickedness cease upon its face."[7]

Thus, according to modern revelation,

> Satan shall be bound, that old serpent, who is called the devil, and shall not be loosed for the space of a thousand years. (D&C 88:110)

The millennial binding of Satan and his followers will not be the result of some magical incantation from the eternal worlds, but rather a simple function of the force of virtue.

> *And because of the righteousness of his [the Lord's] people,* Satan has no power; wherefore, he cannot be loosed for the space of many years; for he hath no power over the hearts of the people, for they dwell in righteousness, and the Holy One of Israel reigneth. (1 Nephi 22:26; italics added)

The shackling of Satan through individual righteousness needn't be postponed until the Savior comes. This personal millennium may begin anytime. As we choose the right in our own lives, it will be brought to pass—one person at a time.

However, when the Savior does come to "subdue all enemies under his feet" (D&C 76:61), the Millennium of peace ushered in by him will be universal. It will be like no other period of this earth's history.

> And they shall beat their swords into plowshares, and their spears into pruninghooks: nation shall not lift up sword against nation, neither shall they learn war any more. (Isaiah 2:4)
>
> The eyes of the blind shall be opened, and the ears of the deaf shall be unstopped. Then shall the lame man leap as an hart, and the tongue of the dumb sing. (Isaiah 35: 5–6)
>
> And the work of righteousness shall be peace. . . . And my people shall dwell in a peaceable habitation, and in sure dwellings, and in quiet resting places. (Isaiah 32:17–18)

The Savior and his righteousness will reign for a thousand years. We will live in a world without war, hunger, sickness, misery—or the influence of Satan. You can't get better than that. Still, like all good things in the second estate, even this respite from Satan will come to an end.

> And then he shall be loosed for a little season, that he may gather together his armies. (D&C 88:111)

The loosing of Satan will no doubt occur as the Millennium's inhabitants gradually depart from the principles of the gospel. The circumstance will be similar to those described in 4 Nephi, when the Nephites removed themselves, step by step, from the Lord and his teachings. So it will be in the future. Many of God's children will drift, slowly but surely, from righteousness, blessings, and prosperity, into pride and complacency, and eventually to rebellion and wickedness.

According to President Joseph Fielding Smith, the wickedness engulfing the final days will be devastating.

> After the thousand years Satan will be loosed again and will go forth again to deceive the nations. . . . Men will again deny the Lord, but in doing so they will act with their eyes open and because they love darkness rather than light, and so *they become sons of perdition*.[8]

Elder Orson Pratt gives us the details of this tragedy.

> As many as can be influenced by Satan to apostatize will do so . . . and there will be a great division of the people, at the end of the thousand years. . . . He with his army will come against the Saints, and the beloved city, and encompass them round about. His army will be so great that it will be able to come upon the Saints on all sides. . . . Because of the favorable position he is to hold, in that great last battle, and because of the vast number of his army, he doubtless believes that he will get the mastery and subdue the earth and possess it. I do not think he fully understands all about the designs of God.[9]

Indeed, he never did. Satan's undoing has always been his inability to know the mind of God, or to understand what truly motivates God's children. The adversary will never be able to relate to the concepts of love, obedience, faith, or sacrifice—and he cannot comprehend us when we choose the right.

The "battle of the great God" (D&C 88:114) will culminate in the destruction of Satan's kingdom.

> And fire came down from God out of heaven, and devoured them. (Revelation 20:9)

Modern revelation provides us with slightly more detail regarding the defeat of Satan's united forces.

> And Michael . . . even the archangel, shall gather together his armies, even the hosts of heaven.
>
> And the devil shall gather together his armies; even the hosts of hell, and shall come up to battle against Michael and his armies.
>
> And then cometh the battle of the great God; and the devil and his armies shall be cast away into their own place. (D&C 88:112–14)

You and I will be active participants in the battle of the great God under the direction of Michael. But in a very real sense, we already play our parts in that conflict every day. Each time we choose the right, we inch forward to the inevitable victory.

## The Destiny of Satan

The nature and meaning of "their own place" is fairly well known. The scriptures speak of it as outer darkness. Of its embodied inhabitants, the Prophet Joseph revealed,

> And we saw a vision of the sufferings of those with whom he made war and overcame: . . .
>
> Thus saith the Lord concerning all those who know my power, and have been made partakers thereof, and suffered themselves through the power of the devil to be overcome, and to deny the truth and defy my power—
>
> They are they who are the sons of perdition, of whom I say that it had been better for them never to have been born;
>
> For they are vessels of wrath, doomed to suffer the wrath of God, with the devil and his angels in eternity; . . .
>
> These are they who shall go away into the lake of fire and brimstone, with the devil and his angels—
>
> And the only ones on whom the second death shall have any power;
>
> And, verily, the only ones who shall not be redeemed in the due time of the Lord, after the sufferings of his wrath. (D&C 76:30–33, 36–38)

Descriptions of outer darkness are sparse but nonetheless vivid.

> Wherefore, he saves all except them—they shall go away into everlasting punishment, which is endless punishment, which is eternal punishment, to reign with the devil and his angels in eternity, where the worm dieth not, and the fire is not quenched, which is their torment—
>
> And the end thereof, neither the place thereof, nor their torment, no man knows;
>
> Neither was it revealed, neither is, neither will it be revealed unto man, except to them who are made partakers thereof. (D&C 76:44–46)

Elder Joseph Fielding Smith explains why this hell is such a dismal place.

> Outer darkness is something which cannot be described, except that we know that it is to be placed beyond the benign and comforting influence of the Spirit of God—banished entirely from his presence.[10]

So the ultimate dwelling place for Satan and his rebellious hosts will be a kingdom of darkness, a degree devoid of glory, since glory is precisely what they are not prepared to endure.

Beyond this point, nothing has been revealed of Satan and his followers. We know that intelligence cannot be created or made, and assume it cannot be destroyed. Scientifically we are told that matter and energy possess this same indestructible quality. But do these damned beings—having rejected all light—qualify as matter, energy, or intelligence as we understand them? Elder John A. Widtsoe does give a sobering thought with one last glimpse of these individuals.

> The final end of such beings is not known. As they are eternal, it is doubtful if they can ever fully destroy themselves. Nevertheless, as they oppose law, they will at last shrivel up and become as if they were not.[11]

## Notes

1. Joseph Fielding Smith, *Doctrines of Salvation*, comp. by Bruce R. McConkie (Salt Lake City: Bookcraft, 1954–56), 3:315.

2. Ezra Taft Benson, "In His Steps." address at the Southern California Student Devotional, February 8, 1987, 1.

3. James J. Hamula, "Winning the War against Evil." *Ensign,* Nov. 2008, 52.

4. Joseph Fielding Smith, comp., *Teachings of the Prophet Joseph Smith* (Salt Lake City: Deseret Book, 1938, 204–5. (Italics added.)

5. James E. Faust, "The Forces That Will Save Us." *Ensign*, Jan. 2007, 9.

6. Thomas S. Monson, "Correlation Brings Blessings." *Relief Society Magazine,* April 1967, 247.

7. Smith, *Doctrines of Salvation*, 1:83.

8. Ibid., 1:87. (Italics added.)

9. Orson Pratt, in *Journal of Discourses* (London: Latter-day Saints' Book Depot, 1854–86), 18:346.

10. Smith, *Doctrines of Salvation*, 2:220.

11. John A. Widtsoe, *A Rational Theology* (Salt Lake City: Deseret Book, 1952), 83.

# Conclusion
# Fear Not, Little Children

In the meantime, the world we live in is a very telestial one, and Satan is still "abroad in the land" (D&C 52:14). Every day we may look around, read the headlines, and watch the news to observe his methods on parade. It is also easy to see him at work in our lives. What is perhaps most interesting to note is that, in spite of his pretended creativity, all things considered, Satan has not changed all that much.

A few years ago I attended a traditional Latter-day Saint university somewhere on the Wasatch Front. I was serving as elders quorum president and had arrived at my apartment quite late one night after a very busy Sunday. All my roommates had gone to bed, and I sat alone in the kitchen, winding down with a glass of milk, when the telephone rang.

I answered it and immediately sensed something dark and oppressive. It seemed to emanate from the receiver. It was one of the oddest sensations I'd ever felt in my life. I tentatively put the phone to my ear and said, "Hello." And from far away I heard a tiny voice say, "Steve?"

Now I knew that voice. Diana was a sweet, dear friend with an innocent, guileless heart. I said, "Diana, what's wrong?"

She answered, "I'm really scared."

I didn't hesitate. I said, "Diana, wait there. I'll be right over."

Hanging up the phone I raced across the complex, bounded up two flights of stairs to the girl's apartment, and knocked on the door. When it opened, the same oppressive aura flooded through the entryway, smothering me. And Diana stood there in the darkness.

I walked in without an invitation. "Diana," I asked, "what's going on here?"

"I don't know," she answered, "but I'm so frightened."

She should have been. She was alone, or seemingly so, in that suffocating environment. Every light in the apartment was turned off. It was incredibly eerie. I said, "Let's do something first of all." Together we began to turn on every light in the place. We turned on desk lights, closet lights, even the light over the stove. "There," I said, "that will help. But there's more to this than just darkness. Tell me what's happened tonight."

And she did. She'd been with friends, talking and telling stories—*those* stories. And when the evening was over, she and the boy who gave her a ride home continued to discuss the dark side. I think we've all done it. It's fascinating, but fruitless. They invited a malevolent spirit into their conversation. And when she said good night, that powerful spirit came home with her. It was there in that apartment, and we both felt it.

She asked, "Would you cast it out or give me a blessing?"

"In a minute," I said as I sat her down on the couch. "But first, let's talk. Let's talk about the God that you and I worship, and his Son Jesus Christ. That Son is Jehovah of the Old Testament. He created worlds without number, formed the mountains of the earth and the waves of the sea, and causes the nations of men to rise and tumble at his will. This is He who came to earth to literally conquer sin and death, and who holds the power of the universe in His hands—and will willingly share that power with you and me through our faith and through the priesthood—because He loves us.

"Now let's talk about Satan—Lucifer, son of the morning, who once stood in the very presence of the Almighty with all the blessings of time and eternity within his reach. And then through his own pride, greed, and wicked stupidity, let it all slip through his fingers and—losing everything—was cast out. He is today the most miserable loser of all time in this vast universe and spends his existence frightening little girls in the dark.

"Now I want you to compare these two—Jesus Christ, the Savior and hero of your life, and the devil—and ask yourself, 'Do you have anything to fear from Satan?'"

She looked at me. And with revelation beaming from her countenance, she smiled, shook her head slightly, and said, "No."

"Good," I said. "Well, let's give you a blessing." As I did, we were enveloped in peace. We felt the warmth of the Holy Ghost. When she opened her eyes, the spirit of darkness was gone. But then, it was gone before we started, wasn't it?

Satan is real. But Jesus Christ is also real. And there is no comparison between the two. We have been endowed with knowledge, and power, and the capability to drive Satan from our lives, if we will but cling to the Savior. He is our champion.

> And by giving heed and doing these things . . . the kingdom is given you of the Father, and power to overcome all things which are not ordained of him. (D&C 50:35)

> Fear not, little children, for ye are mine, and I have overcome the world, and you are of them that my Father hath given me. (D&C 50:41)

> Wherefore, I am in your midst, and I am the good shepherd, and the stone of Israel. He that buildeth upon this rock shall never fall. (D&C 50:44)

We have his promise:

> Peace I leave with you, my peace I give unto you. . . . Let not your heart be troubled, neither let it be afraid. (John 14:27)

# Sources

## Books

Andrus, Hyrum L., and Helen Mae Andrus. *They Knew the Prophet*. Salt Lake City: Bookcraft Inc., 1974.

Burton, Alma P., and Clea M. Burton. *Stories from Mormon History*. Salt Lake City: Deseret Book, 1960.

Calhoun, Margie. *Stories of Insight and Inspiration*. Salt Lake City: Bountiful Press, 1993.

Calhoun, Margie. *When Faith Writes the Story*. Salt Lake City: Bountiful Press, 1993.

Campbell, Eugene E., and Richard D. Poll. *Hugh B. Brown—His Life and Thought*. Salt Lake City, Bookcraft, Inc., 1975.

Church Educational System. *Old Testament Teacher Resource Manual*. Salt Lake City: Church of Jesus Christ of Latter-day Saints, 1998.

*Teachings of the Presidents of the Church—George Albert Smith*. Salt Lake City: The Church of Jesus Christ of Latter-day Saints, 2011.

Clark, James R., comp. *Messages of the First Presidency of The Church of Jesus Christ of Latter-day Saints*. 6 vols. Salt Lake City: Bookcraft, 1965–75.

Ford, Henry. *My Life and Work*. New York City: Doubleday, Page and Co., 1922.

*Journal of Discourses*. 26 vols. London: Latter-day Saints' Book Depot, 1854–86.

Lambert, George C. *Treasures in Heaven*. Salt Lake City: Juvenile Instructors Office, 1914.

Lundwall, N.B. *Temples of the Most High*. Salt Lake City: Bookcraft, 1952.

McConkie, Bruce R. *Mormon Doctrine*, 2d ed. Salt Lake City: Bookcraft, 1966.

Nibley, Hugh. *An Approach to the Book of Mormon*. Salt Lake City: Deseret Book, 1988.

Nibley, Hugh. *Since Cumorah*. Salt Lake City: Deseret Book, 1988.

Sill, Sterling W. *Thy Kingdom Come*. Salt Lake City: Deseret Book, 1975.

Smith, Joseph. *History of The Church of Jesus Christ of Latter-day Saints*. Edited by B. H. roberts. 2d ed. rev., 7 vols. Salt Lake City: The Church of Jesus Christ of Latter-day Saints, 1932–51.

Smith, Joseph. *Teachings of the Prophet Joseph Smith*. Selected by Joseph Fielding Smith. Salt Lake City: Deseret Book, 1938.

Smith, Joseph Fielding. *Answers to Gospel Questions*. compiled by Joseph Fielding Smith. 6 vols. Salt Lake City: Deseret Book, 1957.

Smith, Joseph Fielding, *Doctrines of Salvation*. compiled by Bruce R. McConkie. 3 vols. Salt Lake City: Bookcraft, 1954–56.

Talmage, James E., *Articles of Faith*. Salt Lake City: Deseret News, 1899.

Whitney, Orson F. *Life of Heber C. Kimball*. Salt Lake City: Stevens & Wallace, Inc., 1945.

Widtsoe, John A. *An Understandable Religion*. Salt Lake City: Deseret News Press, 1944.

Widtsoe, John A., *A Rational Theology*. Salt Lake City: Deseret Book, 1952.

Young, Brigham, *Discourses of Brigham Young*. compiled by John A. Widtsoe. Salt Lake City: Deseret Book, 1925.

# Articles and Periodicals

Benson, Ezra Taft, "In His Steps." Address to Boise Institute of Religion, November 20, 1983.

Campbell, Beverly, "Mother Eve." *Collegium Aesculpium*, vol. 12, no. 1, 1994.

Clark, J. Reuben, Conference Report, October 1949.

Faust, James E., "The Forces that Will Save Us." *Ensign*, January 2007.

Grant, Heber J., "The Planchette or Ouija Board." *The Relief Society Magazine*, Salt Lake City: January 1920.

Hamula, James J., "Winning the War against Evil." *Ensign*, Nov. 2008.

Hyde, Charles S., Conference Report, April 1926.

McConkie, Bruce R., "Who Is the Author of the Plan of Salvation?" *The Improvement Era*, May 1953.

Monson, Thomas S., "Correlation Brings Blessings." *Relief Society Magazine*, April 1967.

Packer, Boyd K., "Our Moral Environment." *Ensign*, May 1992.

Pratt, Orson, "Power and Eternity of the Priesthood." *The Seer*, 1853.

# Other Sources

Barrett, Ivan J. In lecture notes taken by author, Brigham Young University, December, 1970.

Beaumont, Charles, and Rod Serling. "The Howling Man." *The Twilight Zone*, season 2, episode 5, directed by Douglas Heyes, aired November 4, 1960. Beverly Hills, CA: Cayuga Productions,1964. DVD.

Wilson, Dorothy Clarke, J. H. Ingraham, A. E. Southon, Æneas MacKenzie, Jesse Lasky Jr., Jack Gariss, and Fredric M. Frank. *The Ten Commandments*, directed by Cecile B. DeMille, 1956. Los Angeles, CA: Paramount Pictures, 2013. DVD, 231 min.

# INDEX

**A**

Abraham,  8, 9, 20, 21, 35, 37
accuser,  36, 37. *See also* Satan
Adam,  8, 9, 47, 48, 51, 55, 56
Atonement,  28, 33, 37, 42, 52, 55, 67, 74

**B**

Barrett, Ivan J., "There ain't no Hell,"  6, 17
battle of the great God,  101
Benson, Ezra Taft, now is the day of the devil's power,  96
Brown, Hugh B.,his wrestle with the devil,  89

**C**

Cain,
    enticed with oaths and promises,  61–62
    God encourages to return,  61
    loved Satan more than God,  56, 60
    the perfect dupe,  60
Cannon, George Q.,
    obedience,  58
    Satan would shed our blood,  47
casting out devils,  39, 57, 58, 75–76, 77, 82, 105–107
Christ, Jesus, *See* Jesus Christ
Clark, J. Reuben,
    Satan asked the Father to abdicate,  30
    Satan's plan for saving men in sin,  26
commandments in Eden,  48–49, 50

# N

Nehor, 27, 28, 29, 31, 34
Nephi, on Satan's tactics, 6
Nielsen, Swen C., story of Dick, 31–33
Nixon, Robert, story of casting out evil spirit, 83–84

# O

obedience, 27, 51, 56, 58, 60, 61, 97, 100
Ouija boards, 1, 2, 84–86, 93
Outer darkness, 42, 101, 101–102

# P

Packer, Boyd K., Satan's jealousy of us, 38
Page, Hiram, story of false revelations, 76–77
Paul, the Apostle,
　false apostles, 9
　our wrestle against spiritual wickedness, 7
　prince of the power of the air, 69
　we are not ignorant of Satan, 3
Peace shall be taken, 95
Perdition, 21, 39, 40, 41, 42, 100, 101
Perdition, sons of,
　inability to repent, 39, 40, 41
Phelps, William W., saw the destroyer, 95
possession, 39, 57, 58, 64, 74–75, 83–84, 86, 87, 88, 88–89
Pratt, Orson,
　fallen angels forbidden to multiply, 38
　limits on Satan's power, 74
　on redeeming men in their sins, 27
　Satan's army after the millennium, 100
priesthood of God, 73, 74, 84, 97
prince of darkness, *See* Satan

# R

Rigdon, Sidney,
　being thrown by an unseen power, 56–57

# S

Satan,
　a dangerous egomaniac, 20
　and Adam and Eve's children, 8, 55, 56
　as a celebrity, 19

Index

testing the spirits,  13–14
third of the hosts of heaven,  23, 26, 35, 38
Twilight Zone,  5, 17

## U

unpardonable sin,  39–42

## V

vessels of wrath,  39, 101

## W

War in Heaven,
    nature of the war,  35–36
    our weapons,  37, 52, 60
    test of faith,  37
    the qualifier for mortality,  37
    we risked spiritual death,  37
Widtsoe, John A.,
    end of those in outer darkness,  102
    rebelling against God,  22
    Satan's plan to eliminate of trials,  26
Woodruff, Wilford,
    spiritualist meeting,  84

## Y

Young, Brigham,
    ghosts,  90, 94
    on knowing evil,  3
    on the spirit of revelation,  93
    Satan causes aches and pains,  72
    Satan's curse,  38
    the devil's power is limited,  73
    watching for counterfeits,  10

# ABOUT THE AUTHOR

Stephen J. Stirling was born in Los Angeles, California, and grew up in the southeast LA semi-ghetto of Huntington Park. Graduating from high school in 1970, at the age of seventeen, he received a scholarship to Brigham Young University.

He earned a bachelor's degree in journalism in 1976, and then spent several years wandering America in search of adventure as a professional vagrant. Interspersed through his college career and days on the road, he served a mission in Chile and taught for five years as an early morning seminary teacher in various ports of call.

Stopping in Chicago, he entered the profession of advertising, a field in which he ultimately held many positions with companies from the Midwest to the Pacific coast. He eventually settled in Orange County, California, where he established Stirling Communications and spent fifteen years as a freelance copywriter, scriptwriter, and video producer. His ghostwriting credits include Richard Simmons' *Deal-A-Meal*, and *Where There's a Will There's an 'A.'* Other creative works include *The Ultimate Catalogue* and the comedy album, *Latter-day Night Live*.

In 1994 he was hired by the Church Educational System and relocated with his family to the Phoenix Valley in Arizona, where he has fulfilled a lifelong dream of teaching released-time seminary for the past nineteen years.

He and his wife, the former Diane Leigh, were married in 1981. They have five adult children, two horses, several chickens, and a farm in Adam-ondi-Ahman, Missouri—where they plan to retire someday.